Community, Continuity and Change

New Perspectives on Staten Island History

Community, Continuity and Change

New Perspectives on Staten Island History

Edited by
Michael Rosenfeld
and Charles LaCerra

Pace University Press
New York, New York

Copyright © 1999

Pace University Press
1 Pace Plaza
New York, NY 10038

All rights reserved

Printed in the United States of America

British Cataloging in Publication Information Available

Library of Congress Cataloging-in-Publication Data

Community, continuity, and change : new perspectives on
　　Staten Island history / edited by Michael Rosenfeld
　　and Charles LaCerra.
　　　　　　　　p.　　cm.
　　Selected papers from the conference Continuity,
community, and change, held Oct. 20-22, 1995, at
Snug Harbor Cultural Center, Staten Island, New
York.
　　Includes bibliographical references and index.
　　ISBN 0-944473-46-6 (alk. paper)
　1. Staten Island (New York, N.Y.).--History--
Congresses. 2. New York (N.Y.)--History--Congresses.
I. Rosenfeld, Michael, 1955-　　. II. LaCerra, Charles,
1928-　　.
F127S7C66　1999
974.7'26--dc21　　　　　　　　　　　　　　98-54709
　　　　　　　　　　　　　　　　　　　　　　　　CIP

Contents

Introduction *Michael Rosenfeld*	1
Some Industries on Staten Island in the Nineteenth Century *Charles LaCerra*	7
The History of the Black Church on Staten Island, 1890–1995 *Patricia Gloster-Coates*	17
Staten Island Historians and the Arcadian Myth *Michael Rosenfeld*	33
The Island Image: Reflections and Refractions from Home and Abroad *Charles L. Sachs*	43
Twice Upon an Island Revisited: Another Look at Staten Island's Role in the Landscapes and Planning of Frederick Law Olmsted *Howard R. Weiner*	71
Edward Arlington Robinson: Staten Island Reflections *Diana Gosselin Nakeeb*	81
Fr. John Christopher Drumgoole, Founder of Mt. Loretto	97

John J. Brennan

Sailors' Snug Harbor: A Microcosm of
Turn of the Century New York Politics 111
Geraldine A. Riley

New Brighton: Some Notes on Diversity 125
Richard B. Dickenson

Appendix 129

Notes on Contributors 133

Index 137

> So it cometh often to pass that mean and small things discover great better than great can discover small . . . likewise the nature of this great city of the world and the policy thereof must first be sought in mean concordances and small portions.
> —Francis Bacon
> *The Advancement of Knowledge*

Introduction

Michael Rosenfeld

The writing of local history in the United States is almost four centuries old, dating to William Bradford's 1632 *History of Plimooth Plantation*. For Staten Island, the first known account of its history is the "Brief History of the Settlement of Staten Island," written in 1818 by Peter I. Van Pelt, a 1799 graduate of Columbia College and minister of the Dutch Reformed Church. Although Bradford's history would ultimately find a place in the national canon as a significant text for all students of American culture, both works owed their inspiration to the same didactic and commemorative impulses that animated much early American historical writing. Contemporaries would have seen each work as kindred exercises in literary culture. With the professionalization of knowledge that began to occur in the 1870s (two decades earlier in the sciences) this began to change. The founding of the American Historical Association in 1886 marked the beginning of a major intellectual and professional divide between local historians whose scope was narrow, methods amateurish and training antiquarian, and professionally trained historians who held graduate degrees in history, sought to align their methods as closely as possible with those of the sciences, and investigated the really important questions of national existence. As this paradigm worked itself out over the course of the twentieth century, professional history came to be written by professors with PhDs who were employed by universities while local history came to be seen as the province of well meaning dilettantes and local boosters reading yellowed newspapers in the attics of quaint small town historical societies.

The writing of both local and national history was impoverished by this artificial separation of what are essentially complementary fields of inquiry. Academic historians sacrificed what we have come to see as a truly revealing window on national developments, one which would have enabled them to see more clearly the working out in daily lives and in intimate detail the epic themes they were tracing on the national canvas. In turn, local historians were cut off from the newer theoretical models and questions that were reshaping the writing of American history and recasting some of the fundamental assumptions of the established narrative. As a consequence, the history that they wrote increasingly lacked resonance in a world that had long left behind the ethos of Frederick Lewis Allen's *Only Yesterday*.

Although fortuitous, something of a convergence began to take place in the 1970s and 1980s as a radical transformation in the writing of American history began to work itself out and the new fields of public history and museum education redesigned museums from passive custodians to active interpreters of their collections. Community studies and the new social history began to elevate localities into scholarly prominence while many of the newer subfields of historical inquiry such as women's history and black history brought to the fore many questions previously unasked or dismissed whose answering would require a significant revision of the inherited version of the American past. At the same time, a younger generation of museum professionals sought to forge a more vital and synergistic relationship with the communities they served while making their exhibits more representative and thus more appealing to a broader public.

In a larger cultural sense these developments form part of the background that gave shape to the papers presented in this volume. In 1993, Jane Covell, then director of education at Sailors' Snug Harbor, and Irene Dabrowski, chair of the social sciences division at St. John's University, convened a coordinating committee to organize a conference on local history. Their intention was to use the conference as a means to build bridges between customarily divided publics and institutions. As they envisioned it, the conference would be a locally pioneering collaborative venture between museums, cultural agencies and colleges; but because it would also attempt to foster a kind of civic discourse that drew the public into conversation with the traditional custodians and interpreters of public memory, they imagined more than just another academic conference with professors speaking to professors. They wanted a deliberate effort made to attract a large general audience to a serious public forum examining local history and community identity. With Staten Island withdrawing from the City of New York and becoming an independent city in its own right a real possibility, Covell and Dabrowski believed that such a conference would be a worthwhile venture in public history.

Complemented by a public arts project involving neighborhood-sited installations and programs, the conference took place over a long weekend at the end of October 1995. Seventeen papers were presented in panels organized thematically. (See the appendix for the conference program.) Nine of those papers are presented here. Of those that are not, most were versions of work that had already appeared in print. Irene Dabrowski's "Local Needs and Citizen Leadership," a study of neighborhood community organizations, was in print in a sociology/urban studies reader. William Askins' presentation about Sandy Ground, the historically black community on Staten Island's south shore, was excerpted from his highly informative 1989 CUNY dissertation. Barnett Sheperd's talk on Daniel Tompkins, vice-president of the United States and local real estate developer, was based on a series of superb essays on Tompkins that have appeared over the past several years in the *Staten Island Historian*. Joseph Bongiorno of St. John's University spoke about the history of the railroad on Staten Island, offering an expanded version of the undergraduate thesis he presented at St. Francis College. Work on the early history of Staten Island by Randall Brown, an independent scholar who is a graduate of Wesleyan's American Studies program, is now appearing in the *Staten Island Historian*. Albert Melniker, the distinguished local architect, spoke anecdotally about his youth on Staten Island in the 1920s and 1930s and offered a professional perspective on the course of the Island's development, including observations on the local impact and legacy of Robert Moses, but declined to put his reminiscences in writing. There were also presentations by Anthony Haynor of Seton Hall University on the ethnic history of the predominantly

Italian community of Rosebank and Harvey Weber of St. John's University on Sailors' Snug Harbor and 19th century homelessness. Most of the presentations were videotaped for the archives of the Staten Island Institute of Arts & Sciences.

The essays included in this collection all make a significant contribution to the writing of Staten Island history. They help to expand the traditional narrative scripting its past by bringing to the writing of its history the newer methodologies current in museum studies and the various academic disciplines. As a result, they call attention to a more complex past than the one presented in many of the earlier histories, offer a fuller sense of local history by meaningfully incorporating excluded or marginalized people into the story, and highlight the continuing tension between perspective and perception—what you see depends upon who and where you are—in the creation of a community's sense of itself.

Where these essays differ most notably from the established narrative, and this in itself is a significant theme lending unity to the work, is in their sense of Staten Island being located fully within the orbit of the larger metropolitan region and from its earliest days having to respond to events taking place in that larger world. Implicitly or explicitly, the authors in this volume reject the traditional conception of "splendid isolation" that saw Staten Island as a separate and sylvan paradise rudely hustled into the urban horrors of the late twentieth century with the opening of the Verrazzano Narrows Bridge in 1964. Charles LaCerra's essay in economic history shows how, for example, by the mid-nineteenth century the Island's economy was being transformed by nationally oriented industrial concerns, observing in passing how a preindustrial activity, oystering, was destroyed by a twentieth century problem, water pollution. Making use of different sources, both Michael Rosenfeld and Charles Sachs explore the process by which a community's identity is created and how that identity then becomes an exploitable and marketable commodity used by various constituencies for their own economic and political ends. Geraldine Riley demonstrates in a fine foray into the new political history that progressive reform, so salient a feature of public life in turn-of-the-century America, had local manifestations and consequences. In another form that can also be seen in John Brennan's study of Fr. John Drumgoole which draws connections between religious charity, child welfare, and urban social reform at the end of the last century. Stepping back one generation, Howard Weiner, in a provocative essay on Frederick

Law Olmsted, shows how the landscape of Staten Island entered into Olmsted's patrician vision of orderly and planned communities as an antidote to the chaotic disorder of industrialization and urbanization. How Staten Island reconfigured the imaginative landscape and altered the poetic vocabulary of the distinguished poet Edward Arlington Robinson is ably documented by Diana Nakeeb in a splendid essay that connects physical terrain and cerebral journeys. Lastly, Patricia Gloster-Coates and Richard Dickenson each address aspects of race in relation to local identity, bringing into prominence the long African-American presence on Staten Island. Dickenson, focusing on a single neighborhood, draws a hopeful parallel between Irish/Italian assimilation and political ascent in previous generations with the expectations of today's African-American community; and Gloster-Coates, in a wonderfully pioneering essay in local religious history that moves well beyond the traditional parameters of standard church history, explores the history of the black church in Staten Island in relation to local needs as well as some of the larger questions confronting the black church in the United States.

Nineteen-hundred ninety-eight marks the one hundredth anniversary of the five boroughs joining together in the Metropolitan Compact to form Greater New York. These essays demonstrate that for better or worse Staten Island has been intimately involved in the development of New York City. They call attention to a rich and complex history and implicitly suggest ways to enrich further our understanding of that history. Different kinds of evidence (visual, written, monumental), cultural approaches exploring memory and investigating meaning, religious history that places churches in the world, work(er) culture, the new political history, community and ethnic studies: all hold out the possibility, especially when they are deployed as foreground illuminating background and throwing it into relief, of helping to expand the narrative of local history and enriching a community's understanding of itself. While speaking directly to Staten Island's history, the essays here speak as well to the history of Greater New York. Although separated physically from the metropolis, the issues and challenges confronting the metropolitan community have long played themselves out in local variations among the people of Staten Island. Their lives and heritage resonate with meaning for all who are interested in the past or how that past can be written.

Richmond Turnpike (now Victory Blvd.) Looking north towards Tompkinsville, ca. 1900. Courtesy Staten Island Historical Society.

Some Industries on Staten Island in the Nineteenth Century

Charles LaCerra

America before the Civil War was largely agrarian, with over eighty percent of the population living in rural areas, farms and small villages. This general picture also characterized Staten Island with its picturesque hills, shaded valleys, grand old forests, beautiful sea-girt, and costly villas. From the early years of the 19th century, Staten Island's main industries were farming and fishing. By the third decade of the century, however, the Island began to lose its strictly rural cast. Those who believed in New York's bright future saw the development of Staten Island as bright and promising. It lay at the threshold of one of the greatest cities of the world, and it is no wonder that its beauty and resources attracted home seekers and entrepreneurs.

The British, during their colonial eminence in America, had placed restrictions on manufacturing and the development of industries. By the middle of the 19th century, when the British dominance had long been removed, the states were still living in the shadow of those restrictions, which retarded the development of some industries by a generation or so. Nevertheless, by the 1850s a number of industries operated on a wide scale throughout Staten Island, bringing prosperity to its small population. It is the contention of this paper that industries grew on Staten Island despite its industrial lag, and that the Civil War acted as a stimulus rather than a deterrent to the commerce of some industries.

Perhaps one of the most famous names among the manufacturers in Staten Island's history is that of Balthasar Kreischer, renowned for his brick making. In 1836, Kreischer migrated from Germany to New York City, where he founded a brick factory in partnership with one Charles

Mumpeton. Kreischer had been trained in Hornbach, Bavaria, as a brick maker and, after learning about the devastating fire in New York City in December of 1835, decided he could help rebuild the city. In 1845, his Manhattan firebrick works were using New Jersey clay. When he discovered that these clay beds extended to Staten Island, he investigated a site and by 1855 had built his first factory on Staten Island.

Kreischer also founded "Kreischerville," where he built two-family houses for his workers, a grocery store, hotel and post office. His own mansion was close by on the southwestern shore of the island, near Staten Island Sound. The development lasted until 1883, when the factory, mansion and housing were all destroyed by fire. However, this successful industry and family business did not to come to an end until well into this century.

Kreischer excavated clay principally by steam dredging of river beds. Clay material was thrown on the banks in order to dry. The clay, before drying was unctuous, natty and smelly. Soon its water dried out and it had to be re-dug. From the banks it was carted to tempering pits, where water was added. Several horses turned a wheel to draw sufficient water for this stage. The softened clay was then shoveled from the pits and transported to the molding bench, if molded by hand, or to the machine, if shaped by machine . Here the clay was molded into bricks. The clay, in molds, was then placed on trucks to be taken to the yard for drying.

After the bricks were dry, edges were hacked and spatted to smooth their shape. They were then brought to the kiln for burning, or the banking process. After burning and cooling, the bricks were placed in wagons or cars for shipment to their destination. This method remained satisfactory until manufacturers conceived of additional machines to expedite the process.

What came to be known as "The Machine Method" was costly, but produced cheaper bricks in the long run. In this method, brick-shaping mechanisms were mounted on a scow as part of the dredging operation. In one continuous operation the clay passed through the mixing and molding process into completely formed bricks, ready for drying and burning. All this was done by machinery, automatically. Only a small crew was needed on the scow to operate the machinery. The new machinery deepened the channel at the same time that it excavated the clay.

In the *Richmond County Sentinel* of August 28, 1886, an obituary appeared on the first page titled "Kreischerville's Founder-His Death at

His Residence on Wednesday Evening-A Sketch of His Busy and Useful Life-He Leaves Great Riches and A Good Name which is Far Better." The article cited Kreischer's entrepreneurship and ingenuity in using the Island's resources to meet the demands of a domestic market for bricks. (Bricks imported from England were no longer desirable as they were warped and unfit for use by the time they arrived in America.) In addition to building a business that was to remain in family hands, part or all, Kreischer was one of the original trustees of the Dry Dock Savings Bank and helped originate the Staten Island Railway.

A prospectus titled "Boston Anderson Company Prospectus 1887" described a new method of brick making which the Anderson Company was using in Chicago. Numerous patents had been registered by the Kreischer Family. Now George, Balthasar's son, joined the syndicate to produce bricks as a subsidiary of New York Anderson. As a syndicate, they could share patents. Extant documents indicate that George bought at least $33,000 in shares in Anderson's Company.[1] Together, they were very successful.

Of special interest among industries of the 1850s is oystering. It seems the oyster industry went well back to the early 18th century, since legal history shows an attempt to regulate the gathering of shellfish by 1715. The boundaries of the shore lines and adjacent waters were in a confused state because of the imprecise grants made to the Duke of York in 1674 by Charles II of England. The Duke was given the whole of the Hudson River. New Jersey and Pennsylvania, it seems, had their territories marked off at low tide, giving rise to confusion over shore rights. Instruments and mapping also were less accurate than they are today.[2] New York, hence, persisted in its claims after the American Revolution, when a number of states almost went to war over territorial disputes.

Consequently, there were a number of oyster wars, especially between New York and New Jersey. Residents of Prince's Bay planted larger quantities of oysters and tried to prevent their removal by New Yorkers. Some boatsmen of Mariner's Harbor met in 1856 at Bull's Head to claim public rights in Prince's Bay. The residents also claimed rights in the area inasmuch as they cultivated the beds.[3]

A Joint Commission from New York and New Jersey was established to set boundaries. It gave exclusive rights to Staten Island east of a line drawn from Prince's Bay to Sandy Hook. To the north, Staten Island was cut off from exclusive rights to Newark Bay. Rather the Commission declared the center of Kill Van Kull and Staten Island Sound as the dividing line. Staten Island lost much of her fishing rights.

This decision, however, did not end the conflict. But when the Civil War started in 1861, a new dimension was added. Trade between Staten Island and Virginia had gone on before the War. Now northern schooners and sloops were being seized. Reports came to Staten Island of hostile gangs along the Virginia shores bearing arms.[4] Virginians needed trade with Staten Island to support themselves, but the War created mistrust and numerous other outrages against both Yankee and Confederate oyster men. However, the War acted as a stimulus to northern industries as northern markets were cut off from the South.

All along the Atlantic coast, from Massachusetts to Georgia, lay rich oyster beds. Harvesting them was an intensive industry that ran into the tens of millions of dollars and involved the use of thousands of boats. The tastiest oysters were cultivated in northern waters to mature and improve their flavor and value since warmer waters produced less tasty and flabby ones. Bivalve oysters produced off the Staten Island coast were considered the best and stood up well against the coppery-flavored English and other tasteless varieties. The New York season lasted for nine or ten months and the *Richmond County Gazette* of November 5, 1873 estimated the wholesale industry to be worth $40 million. Some 10,000 to 17,000 people were employed in New York Harbor to produce these juicy bivalves. Many businessmen working their industries from their seaside mansions in Staten Island, became known as oyster-millionaires.[5]

During the 1850s, attempts to keep the beds clean for cultivation were reported. Scrapers like scythes dragged along the floor of the sea and pulled the debris up in ring-like iron purses. The scourings were then put on boats and later thrown overboard into the current. It was a tedious job, done under full sail. The depth of water the dredgers worked in was 8 to 25 feet. It was into these waters that Virginia oysters were planted. The Civil War, however, turned Staten Island's industry into planting for homestock.[6]

After the War, businessmen on the Island were still very upset about the tampering with the beds. The *Richmond County Gazette* in 1871 ran an ad by the Oyster Planters' Association of Richmond County announcing a meeting for all concerned planters to determine if the oyster watch "in the lower section of Princess Bay near Great Kills shall be continued during the next three months."[7] The watch would have to be discontinued if no action were taken. So, with a shrinking industry because of shrinking beds, the planters formed vigilante groups to protect their interests.

Apparently not only boatsmen from across the Sound stole oysters from the Staten Island waters, but also native Islanders. Local residents would enter the beds, especially at low tide, and help themselves to oysters. Local planters, however, tended to look the other way and not prosecute these people. It was big thieves they were trying to curtail.

Oyster beds became further depleted by the next decade, but for different reasons. In an article titled "To Save The Oyster Beds," the *Richmond County Gazette* reported on August 7, 1886 that the Oyster Inspector had been accumulating evidence against certain companies polluting the water around Staten Island. The Inspector was watching Bayonne and the New Jersey shore and recorded the sludge dumped into the Kill Van Kull. Standard Oil Company was the big offender. Apparently Staten Island was contributing to the demise of its own stock also, as industries at New Town Creek were depositing oil and other kinds of sludge in the water. The Oyster Inspector said his office would try to prosecute.

Staten Islanders often used the rivers of New Jersey, the Passaic and Hackensack, to give oysters a "drink." But later, New Jersey passed laws against this. By 1860, boatsmen were using submerged floats to give the oyster a drink, or chance to cleanse themselves. Complaints of pollution killing the oyster industry, however, continued. In 1910, a number of typhoid cases were attributed to oysters from the region, which forced New York wholesalers to abandon the local market. By 1916, the Department of Health condemned the oyster beds on Staten Island. Waste products of other industries had destroyed an industry that employed thousands and supplied a rich source of protein.[8] Laws against pollution were ineffective.

Sadly, an industry that blossomed in mid-century was allowed to die by leaders with little foresight. A plentiful supply of seafood that grew in the surrounding waters of New York Harbor was poisoned, ending a rich supply of inexpensive food and eventually driving the price of seafood higher than the price of some meat products.

As well known as the oyster enterprise on Staten Island was the dyeing industry. The New York Dyeing and Printing Establishment, located at Factoryville in New West Brighton, dated back to 1819. The firm's work consisted of dyeing, printing and refinishing dress goods and other textile fabrics. This factory was started by Colonel Nathan Barrett, and others, and became well-known throughout the world. But by the middle of the century, Barrett wanted out so he could update and innovate factory processes.[9]

In 1851, Colonel Barrett along with his nephews, Nathan, Joseph and Edwin Heal formed the "Barrett, Nephews and Co.'s Fancy Dyeing Establishment." These men invested $24,000, half of which was financed by Barrett. The site of the new plant was on Cherry Lane, in Castleton, about a mile south of Port Richmond, and only a short distance from New West Brighton.[10] The Venture proved profitable right from the beginning and profits were returned immediately to the business to enlarge the buildings and install new machinery. Barrett, a restless man, traveled to Europe to examine dyeing establishments to see what profitable information he might gain for his own needs.[11]

A large part of Barrett's production concerned the dyeing and finishing of "grey" goods, fabric that had never been dyed or finished before. In this class were dress goods, French cashmeres, merinos and elaines, and in veilings, parisinas, baregas, and velveteens, and so on. The availability of abundant water on Staten Island helped promote the industry. The company reached a high point of perfection comparable to the Europeans. Barrett employed about 400 people on his acre and a half enterprise.[12] Bayles noted in 1887 that Barrett and nephews "developed so rapidly, and in so many different directions, that at present its claim to be considered second to no other concern in this line of business in the country is generally conceded."[13] Barrett had achieved the eminence he desired for his company, but unfortunately did not live to see it recognized as such.

The New York Dyeing and Printing Establishment continued to employ close to 500, enjoying a large share of the market on the eastern seaboard. But it restricted its production to dyeing cotton goods and the manufacture of bookbinders' cloth. The Old Dyeing Establishment, as it came to be known, cleaned and dyed ladies and gentlemen's clothing, but never developed the skill of Barrett's brainchild to create fine fabrics.[14] By the end of the century it declined as a major producer on Staten Island.

Another local industry of great proportions was beer-making. Local historians say that breweries first made their appearance on Staten Island in 1851. Some credit Giuseppe Garibaldi and Antonio Meucci with having established the first still, while others say it was only their names that were used to promote the venture.[15] During 1848, revolutions continued to unsettle Europe and hundreds of refugees, especially Germans, settled around Stapleton and Clifton.[16]

Stapleton, the center of brewing, had by 1859 become the most important village on the east shore of the Island. The Island was an ideal place to make beer as it had a plentiful supply of fresh water needed for brewing; necessary ingredients were also grown on Staten Island. To the west, rimming Stapleton, were caves that could provide cool and safe winter storage, caves once used by Hessian troops during the Revolutionary War. The first beer-making venture was established near Vanderbilt Ferry Landing and was called Clifton Brewery. After several owners, Frederick Backmann acquired the factory originated by Meucci and his brew became quite popular.[17]

In 1853, another brewery was established by one John Bechtel, also in Stapleton, near what is now Broad and Van Duzer Streets. Village roads at the time were poor or nonexistent, so the company had to stable their horses in New York City. A ferry brought them back and forth when they were needed for delivery. Later, when Bechtel enlarged his operations, he set up unusual stables for his 72 truck horses. They were two-storied structures, fireproof with iron beams and a tiled floor. In addition, Bechtel's son George built a hospital for sick horses, elegant offices and a Russian bath laid in cement with white and blue tiles.

In 1850, a Mr. Wolfe, of Engel and Wolfe of Philadelphia, founded the largest lager beer brewery in the Stapleton area. In 1870, Rubscam and Hormann purchased it. At the Centennial Exhibition in 1876, eleven gold medals were awarded breweries in the United States. Of these eleven, Bachmann, Bechtel, and Rubscam and Hormann won three. But it was Bechtel who drew international praise for his product. In 1878, the company received an award from the Paris Exhibition, and the following year, a prize at the Sidney Fair in New South Wales. Praise for Bechtel's beer came from many quarters.[18]

The Bechtel family had made quite a name for itself above and beyond their business prowess. George Bechtel became the most famous. Born in Germany in 1840, George became prominent in the area after taking over his father's business. He rebuilt the business and introduced electric lighting to Staten Island. George became a wealthy and charitable man, yet he retained some of those revolutionary roots that brought his countrymen to these shores. When abolition became a hot issue at the time of the Civil War, he protected blacks after riots broke out in the area. Blacks stayed in the woods while Bechtel provided them with food until things quieted down. Bechtel was also responsible for starting the first hospital on Staten Island, the S.R. Smith Infirmary, now the Staten Island Hospital. Lincoln named George Ambassador to Luxemburg. Unfortunately, this imaginative and kind man died prematurely in 1899.[19]

Walling's map of 1859 shows that Bechtel also had a beer garden, a cultural transplant from Germany, at Broad and Van Duzer streets. The beer garden was a place to socialize, meet friends, enjoy a few songs, and dance. Walling's map also shows a Mr. Schmidt's brewery at Four Corners, Castleton. There was a Schafer's brewery in Stapleton during the 1850s. Whether or not these producers were predecessors of the present day Schafer Company is not possible to ascertain.[20]

On February 21, 1883, the *Richmond County Sentinel* reported that five large brewers existed on Staten Island in the Stapleton-Clifton area.[21] It named Rubscam and Hormann, Frederick Bachmann, Monroe Eckstein, and Charles Bischoff. It noted that brewing was a million dollar business and the largest on Staten Island. Plant operations were worth more than a million and a half, and the money relayed to the industry circulated rapidly. At this time, brewers were at odds with the operators of the Staten Island Railroad and Ferry Service. Transportation was costly, as it was for many industries dependent upon the rails to get their product to market. In addition, the SIRR refused to put extra boats in service so that deliveries could get to their destinations on time.

Later, to survive, many of these breweries merged. By 1914, the clatter and clop of horses and the rumble of iron-tired beer trucks gave way to motor trucks making deliveries. But changes came all too late to save these producers. When Prohibition was enacted, the beer companies tried to convert to other purposes to survive and to relieve the unemployment that resulted. Rubscam and Hormann tried to manufacture artificial ice and cereal beverages. Dorothy Valentine Smith pointed out in her history of Staten Island: "The old Bechtel-Bachmann plant was used for a variety of operations till badly damaged by fire in 1931."[22] Rubscam and Hormann was remodeled after prohibition and was successful for 21 more years, until Piel Brothers bought control in 1954. They held control until 1963, when operations on the Island were discontinued. A multimillion dollar industry had come to end.

One industry of more modest proportion on Staten Island was basket-making by local farmers. It was characteristic of *ante-bellum* farming. The production of baskets preceded the coming of colonists, as the Indians had two reservations when they sold Staten Island and they used ash and hickory wood to make baskets. Black ash was also used by white men for basket-making as the bark was easily removed. Many other kinds of saplings lost their bark after soaking. A wood beetle was then used to hammer out the branches and twigs.[23] The farmers wove on rainy days and between crop cultivation.

The tools used for basket-making were the shaving horse, draw knife, measure stick, felling ax, wedges, wooden mallets and beetles. Eight foot stripped saplings were used for the sidings, and six foot strips for the hoops. Four foot strips were used for the ribs. During the 1850s, oyster bushel baskets sold for 50 cents. During the war, business continued and basket prices went up to between 80 and 90 cents a basket. Two by three bread baskets sold for $2.00 each and a baker's wagon basket, four by eight, sold for $8.00.[24] By the measure of the day, these baskets were not cheap. The domestic production of these items helped many farmers survive by carrying them over seasons of poor crops.

During the 19th century, many other industries thrived on Staten Island, although it remained largely rural, and suburban to New York City. Industries, some with deep historical roots, engaged thousands of residents and involved millions of dollars. The industries cited here took full advantage of the natural resources of the Island, and notwithstanding the upheaval of the war years, thrived throughout the mid century. Their demise was related to other events and phenomena.

Notes

1. Prospectus 1887 "Boston Anderson C., Prospectus 1887 The State of the Art." Archives. Staten Island Museum, S.I.
2. *The Staten Islander,* July 26, 1856, p. 2.
3. *The Staten Islander,* April 10, 1856, p. 2.
4. *Richmond County Gazette,* May 1, 1861, p. 4.
5. *Richmond County Gazette,* November 5, 1873, p. 1.
6. *Department of the Interior Tenth Census of the United States*

The Oyster Industry by Ernest Ingersoll. Washington: Government Printing Office, 1881. p. 113.

7. January 4, 1871, p. 2.
8. From a paper by Hugh Powell, Librarian for the Staten Island Museum, titled "Princess Bay, Lemon Creek and The Oyster Company," p. 25F. In Achives.
9. J. J. Clute, *Annals of Staten Island From Its Discovery to the Present Time.* New York: Press of Chas. Vogt, No 114 Fulton Street, 1877
10. Richard M. Bayles, *History of Richmond County, (Staten Island)* New York. Edited by Richard M. Bayles, New York: L. E. Preston and Co. 1887.
11. Clute, *op. cit.,* p. 324
12. Clute, *op. cit.,* p. 324
13. Bayles, *op. cit.,* p.726
14. Bayles, *op. cit.,* p.726
15. Dorothy Valentine Smith, *Staten Island Gateway to New York.* Chilton Book Company, Philadelphia, 1970, p. 153.
16. *Ibid.,* p.153
17. *Ibid.,* p.154
18. *Richmond County Gazette,* July 24, 1889.
19. *Staten Island Advance,* July 11, 1965.
20. See Hugh Powell's files from the *Staten Island Chronicle,* Archives, Staten Island Museum.
21. p. 1.
22. p. 156. From brochure titled, "The Damascus Steel and Iron Company" Publisher New York: I. J. Oliver, Steam Printer: Marble Building, 32 Beekman Street, 1859
23. *The Staten Island Historian,* Vol. I, Jan. 1938, No. 1
24. *Ibid.*

The History of the Black Church on Staten Island, 1890–1995

Patricia Gloster-Coates

The African-American Church on Staten Island has contained and nourished African-American culture since the earliest days of colonialism in the thirteen colonies. Traditionally called "The Black Church" because it was born out of separatism, it has been neglected in the major histories of New York City and also of Staten Island. As American historiography has opened the doors to viewing diverse cultures within its geographical boundaries, social historians have discovered new information which expands the amount of information about African-American people in New York City. In the following essay, we shall attempt to present a current and comprehensive history of the Black Church on Staten Island. The term "Black Church" is used as shorthand to connote the African-American Church. In addition, the terms "African-American" and "black" community are often used interchangeably depending on the historical context.

The Black Church, though born out of separatism, expanded its work until it undertook the same tasks of ministering to its parishioners as did the traditional mainstream denominations. The Black Church became the main vehicle for the development of leadership and the promotion of unique cultural programs within the African-American community. It was and still is the intercessor between American social institutions and the African-American community. In spite of its separatist past, the Black Church closely resembles the mainstream denominations in their profile of Church social activities, parochial financial problems, and declining membership in the post-modern, secular age of the late 1900s.

Definitions of the Black Church

The phrase, "The Black Church" evokes conflicting nuances of thought and action among those who call themselves "African-Americans." The generally accepted concept of the Black Church is that of the traditional seven denominations which arose in response to the *de facto* segregation in the North after the Revolutionary War and to the *de jure* segregation which started in 1896.

Even though as many as 5,000 black men fought to defend the American colonies, they were not accorded equality in social matters. After the Revolutionary War, African-Americans underwent the dumbfounding experience of being rejected at worship by former indentured servants. In the North, they demanded that the freed slaves should sit in isolated seats away from the rest of the congregation.

The formation of the first black denomination, the African Methodist Episcopal Church, is an excellent example of the necessity for the separatist church. In the early 1790s at Philadelphia, Richard Allen, Absalom Jones, and William White decided to join the congregation of St. George's Methodist Episcopal Church in worship. When they seated themselves in the nave with the general congregation instead of the balcony with the former slaves, the ushers told Allen, Jones, and White to leave the premises. In protest, they left, never to return. Within a few years, Richard Allen started the Free African Society. In 1794, the society became known as the Bethel Church and subsequently was called "the Bethel African Methodist Episcopal Church." It became incorporated as the African Methodist Episcopal Church in 1816.

Another black denomination quickly followed the precedent of the A. M. E. Conference. In 1822, the African Methodist Episcopal Zion Church was begun in Lower Manhattan . The term "Zion" was added in response to the inspirational connotations of the term as it appears in the Old Testament. The new A. M. E. Zion denomination, as it came to be known, also achieved incorporation in 1822. About the same time, several predominantly black congregations sprang up in Lower Manhattan near the Five Points district where most African-Americans lived. The names of the congregations are familiar. St. Phillip's Episcopal Church,

Abyssinian Baptist Church, and Mother Zion A. M. E. Zion Church. A virtual movement of black independent churches gained momentum. Its effects were felt in Staten Island. In 1801, the Stapleton Union A. M. E. congregation began to assemble. By the year 1850, Mount Zion African Methodist Episcopal Zion Church had been founded.

During the mid-1890s, the next wave of separate black denominations surged forth. In the wake of the Supreme Court's Plessy versus Ferguson decision of 1896, black Christians found that *de facto* segregation had become *de jure*. Professor James M. Washington at Union Theological Seminary, New York City, has documented the campaign of black Baptists within the American Baptist Home Mission Society to persuade their white counterparts to oppose vociferously the expanding pattern of racial discrimination. For two main reasons, the black Baptists decided to secede from the mainstream Baptists. First, they were disillusioned by the acceptance of general racial segregation to which their white colleagues had succumbed. Secondly, the black Baptists became vulnerable and fell under the sway of Bishop Henry M. Turner's "Back to Africa" movement which experienced a second awakening during the end of the nineteenth century. Although Bishop Turner belonged to the A. M. E. denomination, he gained an audience in all of the black denominations. In 1895, the black Baptists saw the handwriting on the wall and decided to form the National Baptist Convention, U. S. A. In 1917, this denomination divided in two, producing a second Baptist denomination known as the National Baptist Convention of America, affectionately called "The Unincorporated." The third black Baptist denomination came into being when the disgruntled members of the previously mentioned Baptist denominations found the need for additional inspiration and enlightenment. They gave their new denomination the name, "The Progressive National Baptist Convention, Incorporated," which was incorporated in 1961.[1]

In total, there are seven original African-American denominations which are called historically black. All of them are represented in Staten Island, as will be discussed below. There are three Baptist, three Methodist, and one Pentecostal. The two remaining to be described are the Colored Methodist Episcopal Church which was established in 1870 in the aftermath of the Civil War when the term "Colored" had polite connotations. In response to the growing positive image of African-Americans during the late 1950s, the C. M. E. decided to change its nomenclature to Christian Methodist Episcopal Church. Last, but certainly not least, the Pentecostal denomination is vibrantly represented in the black community by the Church of God in Christ. The black Pentecostal movement swiftly developed[2] in the wake of the Azuka Street movement in California. The date of incorporation was 1894. Only the Progressive Baptists were formed later than this date, as we have previously mentioned.

There is, not surprisingly, a bone of contention as to what the accurate definition of the "Black Church" should be. Data acquired by the writer in interviews, field work, and eminent theological writings indicate that the Black Church has been, as Bertham A. Ogot calls it, "A Place to Feel at Home." When no other institution cared to provide emotional and intellectual solace, the Black Church bore the brunt of separatism. The Church helped to define the African-American corporate personality or "soul" as that of strong persons who have survived long-standing, grim oppression. The clergy and laity see themselves as the preservers and retainers of black culture in the United States.

To quote several prominent members of the historical Black Church, the Reverend Dr. James Terrell, former Chairperson of the Department of Educational Administration at Pace University, said in a recent interview: "The Black Church is a way of life. It is not simply a method of worship." Dr. James Cone, a professor of theology at Union Theological Seminary maintains that the Black Church gave Black Theology its format. Black Theology, which is now taken very seriously, is "an interpretation of faith in the light of black history and culture. It is completely separate from white religion. It is not 'pie in the sky' religion. It is born of a struggle here and now because black Christians refuse to allow oppressors to define who we are."[3]

The Black Church on Staten Island has traditionally followed the national model as a repository of culture and leadership. Its activities and traditions have been recently collated on a historical basis. The Staten Island *Advance* notified the public about the conference on the historiography of the Black Church held in July 1993. Present were the Borough Historian of Staten Island, Richard Dickenson, and members of the Sandy Ground Historical Society. Their goal was to compile a directory of Black Churches solely within Staten Island. A debate arose over the question: Which churches should be considered historically black churches, or simply stated: What is the Black Church? A cross section of

Black churchmen and churchwomen were represented. Featured in the *Advance* article were: Mrs. Lucille Herring of the Sandy Ground Society; Mrs. Yvonne Taylor of Rossville A. M. E. Zion Church; Mr. Richard Dickenson, the Reverend Tony Baker, Deacon Charles Landrum, and Mrs. Evelyn King. The latter person is the historian for the Shiloah A. M. E. Zion Church and also for the National Association for the Advancement of Colored People on Staten Island. Mrs. King defended the historically Black Church. Her point was that only those churches that started out as African-American or black should be included in the proposed directory. "Each church has its own special history, just as individuals do." Other participants disagreed. Dickenson developed a comprehensive definition which was acceptable to the majority of conferees: The Black Church includes the seven historically black denominations, the predominantly black mainstream congregations, and the recently established non-denominational congregations.[4]

With the constantly changing mission of the Church, the definition of the Black Church adopts new and unfamiliar nuances. On Staten Island, the Bethel Community Church was a historically black congregation which withdrew from the A. M. E. denomination in 1942 when the latter refused to finance the building of a new physical plant to accommodate an expanding program. The present rector, the Reverend F. Vincent Cuestas, defines his congregation and similar congregations as "Black Communities within God's Church," not the Black Church.[5] The Reverend Lorentho Wooden, sometime Archdeacon of the Episcopal Diocese of Southern Ohio, believes that the predominantly black congregations within the mainstream denominations have traditionally been more similar in philosophy and activities to the historical Black Church than they have been to the mainstream churches. The logical extension of Wooden's hypothesis is the inclusion of predominantly black congregations in the definition of the Black Church. Otherwise, black Episcopalians, black Methodists, black Presbyterians, and black Reformed churchpersons are left in isolation, rejected both by the Black Church and the mainstream denominations.

As a result of the previously mentioned Conference to assemble a Black Church directory, Dickenson compiled a statistical profile of all the predominantly black congregations on Staten Island. Listed below by region and name, they are:

West Brighton
1. Shiloh A. M. E. Zion Church
2. Mount Calvary Holy Church
3. First Church of God in Christ
4. The Greater New Hope Baptist Church
5. Full Gospel Tabernacle
6. Hall's Temple Church of God in Christ

Mariner's Harbor
7. Fellowship Baptist Church
8. Staten Island Seventh Day Adventist Church
9. St. Phillip's Baptist Church
10. North Shore Church of Christ
11. All Saints Church of God in Christ

New Brighton
12. Good Hope Missionary Church
13. Mount Calvary Church
14. New Direction Baptist Church
15. Pentecostal Faith Church of God
16. Lighthouse Tabernacle
17. Glorious Church of God in Christ

Tompkinsville
18. Bethel Community Church
19. First United Christian Church
20. Saint Paul's Protestant Episcopal Church
(added by the writer based on recent statistics from the archives of the Episcopal Diocese of New York).

Stapleton
21. Stapleton Union Methodist Episcopal
22. First Central Baptist Church
23. Evangel Reformed Church

Clifton
24. Faith Christian Center

Rossville
25. Rossville African Methodist Episcopal Zion Church

Four parishes occupy a special category in their ministry to predominantly black congregations on Staten Island. In the past, the parishes reflected the interests of a predominantly white population. When they left the central city and moved to the suburbs, the clergy of the four parishes decided to remain in the city and reach out to the mixed population in their neighborhoods. During the past ten years, especially, the parishes have expanded and become very prosperous. Listing them alphabetically, they are:

26. Brighton Heights Reformed Church
27. Kingdom Hall of Jehovah's Witnesses
28. Saint Paul's Church of Apostolic Faith of Giving Grace
29. Vanderbilt Avenue Moravian Church.

The ministry that these four parishes have extended to their immediate communities has earned them goodwill and respect and has also guaranteed them a bright future.

Thus, the various ministries by Christian Churches to predominantly black congregations have been chronicled by the Sandy Ground Historical Society and the Borough Historian, Richard Dickenson. The latter's directory provides cartography and vital statistics to illustrate the boundaries and influence of the Black Church in the North Shore and South Central areas at the present time. In defining the Black Church and compiling its directory, the seminal work of the Sandy Ground community, in the past and the present, has to be acknowledged.

The Pivotal Role of the Sandy Ground Community

The southern oystermen who established Sandy Ground as a residential community knew that it would not thrive if it were not centered around a religious institution. In the late 1840s and the early 1850s, family life focussed on the local parish or congregation for a solid example of daily living. Even before the 1840s, there was a significant black presence on Staten Island. J. J. Clute reports in the *Annals of Staten Island* that as far back as 1698, black persons comprised 21 per cent of the total population of 2,847 persons. There were present 594 African-Americans, of whom 10 per cent were slaves and the rest were free.[6]

Askins reports that there were a small number of African-American families living at Sandy Ground before it became attractive to oystermen from Maryland and Virginia. The first African-American who was known for visiting Sandy Ground on a frequent basis was John Jackson who ran his own ferrying service from Clifton, New Jersey to Rossville, Staten Island, and then to Manhattan. We hear of him in local writings around 1850 when he ferried people and goods back and forth to Sandy Ground. The southern free oystermen who thrived after Jackson, then, discovered Sandy Ground while they were employed by Staten Island captains to plant new oysterbeds near Rossville. As their harvests began to flourish, they permanently moved their families from the South to Sandy Ground. In historical writings, their successful venture was brought to public attention by Dr. Minna C. Wilkins in the 1943 volume of the Staten Island *Historian*.[7]

In 1850, the Mount Zion African Methodist Episcopal Zion Church was started by the new residents of Sandy Ground. According to the famous Mr. William Hunter, chronicled in the *New Yorker* magazine of 1959, oystermen from Snow Hill in Maryland, came to Sandy Ground and married into the earliest black families there. In the early 1850s church rosters reveal the names of families who are still prominent at Rossville and Shiloh A. M. E. Zion churches: Purnell, Lamden, Landin, Robbins, Bishop and Henmen. As the fame of the Sandy Ground community spread, black migration into the community increased. Askins reports that there were 149 African-Americans living there in 1880; and that number rose to 196 in 1910. By the latter year, there were also 300 white persons residing there. In 1916, however, misfortune befell the community of Sandy Ground. The New York City Board of Health condemned the oyster beds of Staten Island Harbor as a health hazard due to traces of typhoid bacteria and residual industrial waste. It was incumbent upon the oystermen to move away and seek healthier harbors. Nevertheless, the social institutions of Sandy Ground largely remained intact. Several years before, in 1897, Rossville A. M. E. Zion Church had moved to a new building and resumed the work that the defunct Mount Zion church had left behind. At the beginning of the twentieth century, in spite of encroaching patterns of racial segregation, Rossville set forth on a mission of service to the southern central region of Staten Island.[8]

Congregational Life among the Black Churches, 1890-1940

The separate Black Church was at the zenith of its influence from 1890 through the 1940s. To understand its mission and accomplishments, one must narrate the formation of the six historically black churches which carried on vital ministries to the African-Americans of Staten Island during this important phase.

By far, the oldest congregation is Stapleton Union A. M. E. Church which started in 1801. It was formally established in 1839 and rebuilt in 1923.

Second, Rossville A. M. E. Zion Church came about as a result of the division that occurred at Mount Zion A. M. E. Church in the 1870s. As was mentioned above, the congregation moved into its present building in 1897.

Third, St. Phillip's Baptist Church started as the North Shore Colored Mission in 1879, and then, in 1889 changed its name to Saint Phillip's. In 1966, the entire church congregation and staff relocated from Faber Street to Bennett Street.

Fourth, Shiloh A. M. E. Zion started in 1880. The congregation who broke away from Mount Zion A. M. E. Zion decided to relocate and establish a new parish. It became a mission in 1906 and laid its cornerstone in 1914.

The fifth oldest parish, Bethel Community Church, was called Bethel African Methodist Episcopal Church until the early 1940s. Bethel Church was organized by several women from St. Martin's, West Indies, who despaired over the shortage of Christian programs for the youth of Tompkinsville and Stapleton. As early as the 1890s, the women began holding meetings in their homes. Their audiences were drawn mainly from West Indian migrants and southern African-Americans. By 1909, the new congregation established Bethel Church and incorporated it in 1917. In 1942, the congregation withdrew from the A. M. E. Conference or denomination for reasons we have previously mentioned.[9]

The sixth and last church to be formed was the First Church of God in Christ at Clove Road, New Brighton, which was organized in 1929. For the past sixty-six years, it has nourished its community work without notice until recently when the other mainstream denominations realized that the membership in Pentecostal churches was soaring.[10]

One cannot fully understand the pivotal role the historically black denominations have played in the African-American community from 1890 until the 1940s, unless one reads accounts of church activities from newspapers of that era. Fortunately, the Staten Island *Advance* featured columnists who were sympathetic with the independent spirit and community ministry of the Black Church. What follows is a summary of narrative events which graced the pages of the *Advance* every Saturday in the "Church News" section at turn of the century.

As the central social and religious institution in the community, the Black Church posted a full calendar of social, religious, and fundraising activities. For example, on February 2, 1895, revival meetings were being held at the "Zion Union African Methodist Episcopal Church in Stapleton under the direction of the Reverend Mr. Peterson, pastor, and the Reverend A. F. Johnson of St. Phillip's Baptist Church, Port Richmond." On March 23, 1895, it was further reported that the revival was continuing longer than the planned three weeks due to the overwhelming response from the community. The columnist was elated to report that the entire revival ran for six weeks and paid for itself. In August of 1895, the same congregation, Zion Union in Stapleton, sponsored a fair of crafts. The Ladies Sewing Circle, on this occasion, presented beautiful crafts and cleared the magnificent sum of $100.00.[11] Furthermore, in August of 1895, the parish called Mount Zion Methodist Episcopal Church, as it was designated in the article, held fairs, concerts, and camp meetings. In the spring of 1895, St. Phillip's also held a strawberry and ice cream festival which was a traditional springtime event. The unnamed columnist of the *Advance* frequently commended St. Phillip's for its cultural programs. On December 29, 1894, the parish sponsored a concert of sacred music. At that time, fund raising also took place when the parish asked the audience to make a voluntary contribution for the purpose of augmenting the small annual salary paid to the pastor and his family.[12]

The Staten Island *Advance* of 1900 also yields many colorful descriptions of church activities among the African-American congregations and self-improvement societies. In January, the North Shore Cycle and Benevolent Society gave a concert at St. Phillip's. In October, the Salvation Army gave a concert there; in November, the A. M. E. Zion Church (Rossville) near Pleasant Plains raised money to defray church expenses by sponsoring an ox roast. At the end of the year, a distinguished woman simply referred to as Mrs. Carter from New Orleans gave a lecture about the condition of "colored women" during and after slavery. It was noted in the newspaper that a collection was gathered to defray her travel and speaking engagement expenses.[13]

One social event evoked both excitement and controversy. It was the ox roast. The columnist of the Saturday "Church News" deplored them. Among many parishioners of the various denominations, they were quite popular. Mrs. Evelyn King, the church historian, called the ox roast "the festival of festivals" in her centennial history of Shiloh A. M. E. Zion church. The ox roasts were great social occasions as well as guaranteed fund raising events.[14]

During the 1920s, African-Americans enjoyed the same general economic prosperity as the rest of the population of Staten Island. The amalgamation of Greater New York in 1898 prompted the government of Borough Hall to move its offices from Richmondtown to St. George. Public facilities were quickly constructed to meet growing demands of the population, which increased from 38,000 in 1800 to 85,964 in 1916. Ottley reports that housing conditions among African-Americans of Staten Island compared favorably with those in Flushing and Corona of the borough of Queens.[15] As of 1925, there was a total of 2,206 black persons of whom less than ten percent were immigrants from the West Indies. This group of black persons comprised about 1.6 per cent of the total population of 122,706 citizens and 15,571 resident aliens.[16]

From the 1930s onward, in spite of the Depression, the Black Church continued to increase its membership. Our sources here are Frances Potter's *Church and Communities of Staten Island*, published by the Protestant Council of the City of New York and the National Council of Churches of Christ, USA in 1953, and secondly, the Reverend Jack Burbach's *Report on the Churches of the City of New York* (Port Richmond, Staten Island) published in 1966 by the Protestant Council. From the 1930s until the 1960s, most of the congregations of the Black Church doubled and even trebled their membership. Potter estimated that 1000 African-American Protestants lived in Staten Island by the mid-1950s. This figure included 25 per cent of all African-American residents over age 14 and five per cent of all adult churchmen and churchwomen. The implication is that the African-American population tends to be more active in Church affairs than the mainstream population. In 1966, the Port Richmond reports gave special recognition to St. Phillip's Baptist Church for doubling its membership and providing a broad range of activities for its parishioners. Special recognition was given to the pastor, the Reverend William Epps, for serving actively in community groups like the NAACP, the Urban League and JOIN. St. Phillip's had increased its membership through outreach programs, while some of the mainstream congregations were leaving the neighborhood. Potter notes that mainstream denominations suffered a slight decline in membership after the late 1950s, but they experienced a dramatic 20 per cent decrease in church school enrollment. In 1966, then, the Protestant Council gave special recognition to St. Phillip's Baptist Church for identifying the problems of the community and providing a broad range of programs to work on solutions.[17]

During the 1960s, many social changes took place on Staten Island and they were reflected in the life of the black community. Due to the expansion of public housing apartments, the opening of the Verrazano Narrows Bridge, and the passage of the Freedom of Residence federal law of 1968, a new influx of black residents arrived on Staten Island. At that time, the new opportunities seemed to provide much promise. There were some significant setbacks, though. In 1963, a terrible fire, fed by dry brush, swept southern Staten Island. According to Mrs. Yvonne Taylor, a prominent member of the Sandy Ground Historical Society and the church historian of Rossville A. M. E. Zion Church, Sandy Ground suffered a devastating blow when most of the community residents were burned out of their homes. Many of them subsequently purchased homes in other sections of Staten Island. A few even moved to New Jersey, but the communicants still remain loyal to Rossville A. M. E. Zion Church through faithful attendance.[18]

At the present time, the Rossville Church has the special task of preserving its historic role as the focal point of the Sandy Ground residential community. The leadership of the congregation believe that they have a special obligation to record and narrate all of its history as a predominantly African-American religious and cultural center. In the 1990s, the Rossville Church has been surrounded by new housing developments of condominiums and luxury houses. Where there are now woodlands next to the Church, there soon promises to be additional town houses for the upper middle class. Nevertheless, the congregation intends to provide an outreach ministry to the newcomers as well as to their traditional communicants.[19]

A former historically black church, Bethel Community Church, has the same intentions of providing an effective program to people of its immediate surroundings regardless of ethnic group, religious creed, or national origin. In the mixed neighborhood which lies within walking distance of the Staten Island Ferry, Bethel Church is well known for its effective tutorial and counselling programs for adolescents and young adults.[20] Under the dedicated and experienced guidance of the church leadership team, they are developing new programs which will answer the questions that will be asked at the turn of the twenty-first century.

On Staten Island, and in the nation as a whole, the fastest growing ministries belong to the Pentecostal denomination and the new non-denominational congregations. The historically black churches and the mainstream denominations are growing very slowly in membership. According to Richard Dickenson's directory, the Pentecostals are now the fifth largest denomination in the United States. More alarming than this statistic is the departure of black Christians from the historical black church to the Nation of Islam and the Sunni Muslim Movement. According to Professor Yvonne Haddad, formerly of Hartford University, a large number of African-American men have recently become Muslims. To offset the loss of membership and to retain its central role in the black community, should not the Black Church do away with separatism and establish a new identity of multiculturalism? The Black Church has survived horrendous persecution in the United States. In the next century, it is the mission of the Black Church to teach African-Americans to understand themselves in the broad, international context where "People of Color" constitute two-thirds of the world's population. In this scenario, the African-American will no longer be considered a minority group.

The writer is confident that the Black Church can fulfill its task of defining the African-American identity for the twenty-first century. It has to understand the reasons why the Pentecostal denomination, the non-denominational congregations, and the various Islamic groups have struck a resonant chord in the urban centers of America. To quote the Reverend Mr. Cuestas, "We have to make certain that Dr. Martin Luther King, Jr. did not die in vain." In the same vein, Dr. Nathaniel Jarrett, Jr., President of the A. M. E. Zion Ministerium, declared as he addressed his colleagues, "In about three and one-half years, we will embark into the twenty first century . . . It is time for a change. We need a prophecy, guide, an interpreter, a vision."[21] Surely, the Black Church will meet the challenge.

Notes

1. James M. Washington, *The Frustrated Fellowship* (Macon, Georgia, 1985), pp. vii, 25, 188-189.
2. Stephen Ward Angell, *Bishop Henry McNeal Turner and African American Religion in the South* (Knoxville, Tennessee, University of Tennessee Press, 1992), pp. 217-220.
3. James H. Cone, *For My People: Black Theology and the Black Church* (Maryknoll, New York: Orbis Books, 1984), pp. 19, 61, 207.
4. Tracey Porpora, "When Church is Home," *Staten Island Advance*, Saturday, July 17, 1993, p. B 1.
5. Interview with the Reverend F. Vincent Cuestas, rector of Bethel Community Church, 53 Van Duzer Street, Staten Island. August 15, 1995.
6. J. J. Clute, *The Annals of Staten Island* (New York: Press of C. Vogt, 1877), pp. 70, 329-330.
7. William Victor Askins, "Sandy Ground: Historical Archaeology of Class and Ethnicity in a Nineteenth Century Community on Staten Island" (Ann Arbor: UMI Dissertation Services, 1983), pp. 68, 70.
8. Askins, p. 70; A.Y. Hubbell, *History of Methodism and the Methodist Churches of Staten Island* (New York: Richmond Publishing Company, 1898), pp. 149-153, 159-161; and Joseph Mitchell, *The Bottom of the Harbor*, Little Brown and Company (Boston and Toronto, 1959), pp. 107-108, 112-113.
9. *Bethel Community Church History: Historical Antecedents* unpublished document, church archives 1990 (?), given with permission by the Reverend F. Vincent Cuestas.
10. Richard Dickenson, "Directory of Black Churches on Staten Island (Churches of Color on Staten Island)," unpublished document, private collection of Richard Dickenson, 1994, p. 2. (The entire publication was consulted for dates of establishment.)

11. "Church Note," (Saturday edition), Richmond County *Advance* January 19, 1895; February 2, 1895; March 23, 1895; April 13, 1895; April 20, 1895; August 10, 1895.
12. *Ibid.*, March 17, 1894; June 30, 1894; December 29, 1894.
13. "Church Notes," Richmond County *Advance*, January 26, 1900; October 27, 1900; December 5, 1900.
14. Evelyn M. King, "Shiloh A.M.E. Zion Church Woman's Day Historical Journal, November 30, 1980." Printed by the Royal Press, 1973, Forest Avenue, Staten Island, p. 5.
15. Roy Ottley and Charles Cumberbatch, "Negro in New York," WPA Manuscript, archives of the Schomberg Collection; uses the Laidlaw Census Book of the 1920s, 1936, pp. 4-7.
16. Richard Dickenson and Julie Moody Ojelade, *African-American Vital Records and 20th Century Abstracts, Richmond County, Staten Island.* Published by the Sandy Ground Historical Society, 1985, p. 193.
17. Frances S. Potter, *The Churches and Communities of Staten Island, NY* (New York: The Staten Island Division of the Protestant Council of the City of New York, and National Council of Churches of Christ USA, May 1953), pp. 7, 16, 21-22; *Report on Churches of Staten Island*, The Protestant Council Department of Planning and Research, Staten Island Division, by The Reverend Jack Burbach, 1966, City of New York. Published by the Protestant Council, pp. 8-11.
18. Interview with Mrs. Yvonne Taylor at Rossville A.M.E. Zion Church, Bloomingdale Road, Staten Island, August 17, 1995.
19. *Ibid.*
20. Interview with the Reverend Cuestas, cited above.
21. Nathaniel Jarrett, Jr. "The Value of Visions," *The A.M.E. Zion Quarterly Review*, April 1996 (Vol. VIII), p. 50.

Bibliography

The Caribbean Commission article written by Malcolm Jarues *Proudfoot. Population Movement* in the Caribbean 1950.

Charles Hall. *Negroes in the United States*, 1920–1935. First printed by the U.S. Government Printing office, Bureau of the Census. 1935

Seaton W. Manning. *British West Indians in the United States.* Volume I. Number 5, January 1935. page 27. George Neiones Publications. 71 Harbour Street Kingston, Jamaica.

Reports of the Immigration Commission: Volume I. Abstract of *the Reports* of the *Immigration Commission.* New York: Arno and the *New York Times.* Reprint. 1978. Volume I first printed around 1911.

Joyce Toney. The Development of a culture of migration among a Caribbean people: Sr. Vincent and New York, 1838-1979. Ph.D. 1986 Columbia University.

Harlan Unruh. *Statue of Liberty.* Ellis Island. Volume III. Published by Ellis Island, National Parks administration (p. 839)

Henry Sylvester Williams. *British America.* British Empire Series. London: Kegan, Paul, French and Trubner & Co., LTP. 1900.

Interviews by Patricia Gloster-Coates and Eliz Stevenson

1. Mr. Louis Green of Pittsburgh, Pennsylvania, August 1992
2. Mrs. Undine Nylls Henderson, September 1995.

Interviews from the Ellis Island Oral History Project.

(The numbers used are theirs.)

The Rev. Edward P. Gul. EF 211 Ellis Island Oral History Archives.

Lyle Small #196. (Ellis Island, resources: AKRF interview)

Ayleen Watts James #198. June 25, 1986.

Ellis Island Oral History Interviews #DP 402 Mrs. Vera Clark Ifill, May 23, 1989, Los Angeles.

Mrs. Ella Doroleyne #138, May 21, 1986 Brooklyn, NY.

Staten Island Historians and the Arcadian Myth

Michael Rosenfeld

> God could have created a more beautiful place than Staten Island, but He never did.
> —*George William Curtis*

> Our Slogan: Boost and Boom Staten Island Any Where and Every Where You Go.
> —*Richmond County Democrat-Herald*

> O, Staten Island!—38,507 acres of incongruity and contradiction where the hills are bedrock and the mountains are garbage, and the official flower is either the pinkster azalea or the escaped plastic bag. Staten Island is the land of Kiwanis Clubs and big gas guzzlers for sale on small front lawns, and guys who don't split the check with their dates, and girls who wear high heels at the grocery store and marry young.
> —*Chip Brown*

> Together, We Can Make Staten Island Shine.
> —*Guy V. Molinari*

The Staten Island secession movement, as Senator Marchi wrote in his Summer 1995 legislative report, "has reached its highest benchmark to date." That movement, currently in its twelfth year, is not the first in the Island's history. Entry into the Metropolitan Compact was not universally welcomed in 1898, and attempts to withdraw from it were mounted as early as 1911 and 1916. Then, as now, very much at issue was a sense of self, an almost intangible but nonetheless real sense of place that contributes significantly to how individuals define themselves, characterize their communities, and invest their lives with meaning.

So much of the politics of separatism, as Chip Brown correctly noted in a rather condescending January 1994 *New York Times Magazine* article, has to do with how people see themselves in their everyday lives. For Staten Islanders this has traditionally meant an identity and life-style rooted firmly in the mores and expectations of the small town, home-owning, family-centered, hard-working, blue or pink collar American. Increasingly this world or life-style as well as the very community in which it can be experienced has been perceived as being under attack. "The City," especially its problems, has been seen as encroaching on "The Island" and undermining the kind of life that Staten Islanders supposedly have cherished for generations. Hence the desire to separate from the city.

It would be interesting and instructive if we could enter into the subjective experiences of the 1,505 souls who in 1894 voted against union because they believed the Metropolis across the water was already close enough and that the changes being wrought on Staten Island by proximity "to the second largest city in the world" were not to be welcomed. How would the feelings and thoughts of those now long dead voters compare to those of today who think the city is too much with us? A century ago it was a minority 27% that wished Staten Island to retain its independence; today only 17% voted to retain what 73% of the electorate endorsed in 1894.

The shift in percentages does of course call attention to a question of self-identity. How, one might ask, do Staten Islanders define themselves, and by what means have they arrived at that identity? What forces or factors have provided them with the material with which to construct their own idea of community? Why have they come to see themselves as distinct from the rest of the city? Answering these questions is not easy for what one is trying to do is to give shape to a sensibility, sketch its contours, limn its contents, unravel its origins, and explain its persistence. But understanding how people see themselves is just as important a component of their history as the kinds of houses they build or the types of jobs they hold. Indeed the former will often dictate the latter.

The quotes that introduce this paper span the past century and more-or-less coincide with Staten Island's experience as an integral part of the City of New York. The first quote, almost patrician in tone, dates from about the mid 1880s, a decade after legislative inquiries into metropolitan pute over questions of authority, control and protection. The almost rabid conflict between Peter Stuyvesant and Cornelius Melyn, the Island's third patroon, well sketched in Robinson and Smith's *Staten Island Patroons* (1961), is characteristic. Field Horne, an architectural historian, grasped this point well when he pointed out in *The Conference House Revisited: A History of the Billopp Manor House* (1990) that the Staten Island land grants of Richard Nicholls, the first English governor of New York—recall that the first permanent settlement on Staten Island was made in 1661 and that Nieue Amsterdam fell to the English in 1664—were intended to extend English authority into the island and bring it more closely into the orbit of the metropolis. (It is also important to remember that the early settlement of Staten Island was centered on the south shore, at Oude and Nieue Dorps and the county seat at Richmondtown; the development of the north shore, with St. George as its hub, occurs only during the second quarter of the nineteenth century.)

What is important here is not the notion of the Europeans breaking into a pristine wilderness. That certainly did happen, but I would rather call attention to the fact that from their earliest days of settlement Staten Islanders found themselves involved in complex and strained relations with one another as well as in an ambivalent relationship with the powers centered in Manhattan. Though geography might separate the Island from the mainland and foster, as Leng and Davis point out, a particular variety of insularity, the events and ideas that affected the world sooner or later made themselves felt on Staten Island. Insularity may have bred an "honest simplicity" in the people, but it did not keep them, for example, from discovering, as so many seventeenth century Europeans and Salemites did, witches in their woods. As Ira Morris remarks in volume II of his *Memorial History of Staten Island* (1900),

> And would you believe it—right here on Staten Island witches were punished at the whipping post. Men and women were charged with bargaining with the devil and possessing power to torment whomsoever they pleased. Many believed that the devil was very much like a man in form, only that he had wings, like a bat, a tail, cloven feet, and horns; that he was able to confer great power on witches, enabling them by infernal arts to raise storms, sink ships, afflict children with fits, kill cattle, and set chairs and tables to dancing; that they had power to make themselves invisible, creep through

keyholes, ride on broomsticks through the air, and that it was a special delight to hold their orgies in thunderstorms.

The opening of the Verrazzano Narrows Bridge in 1964 did change Staten Island, but it did not introduce it to the outer world.

Clute was of course uncomfortable with writing about Staten Island as a loyalist stronghold during the American Revolution and in his reticence he may have helped to foster the myth, supported somewhat by Harlow McMillan in his 1976 *The History Of Staten Island, New York During The American Revolution*, that most Islanders secretly cherished the Rebel cause but were intimidated into Toryism by a 30,000 strong British and Hessian force encamped on the Island. This was a ratio of ten soldiers for every resident, intimidating in itself, but McMillan baldly points out that British gold, spent freely, made it much less so.

Here, too, one finds a reiteration of the notion that the Island's insularity cut it off from the great questions of the day and that remoteness bred into the inhabitants an indifference to larger political issues (or to put it another way, fostered narrowness of mind). "The geographical situation of the Island," Clute wrote, "gave direction to the political sentiments of the people." He goes on to add, "There is no evidence that the political questions of the day, which even at this early period began to agitate the minds of the people throughout the several provinces, produced much excitement on Staten Island; the people were an isolated community, holding little intercourse with the world around them, and taking comparatively little interest in matters not of a strictly local character."

McMillan, though offering a more nuanced account of local loyalties than many earlier writers, unfortunately succumbs to the simplistic notion that the Revolution over, there were no hard feelings or public recriminations. He writes, "Whatever the animosities caused by the war, they were not of great significance. . . . Peace, true peace, had come and even the most loyal of the loyalists remaining soon took pride in being a citizen of the independent United States of America, a nation founded on principles of liberty of conscience, equality of opportunity and freedom of expression—principles which Staten Islanders had held to be their birthright long before independence." This is platitude in place of thought and the elevation of patriotic sentiment—the Bicentennial shadowed McMillans' work—over critical inquiry. It also reflects a tendency among post World War II community historians to find (ironically given claims for insularity and isolation!) in the colonial forebears of current Staten Islanders the seeds of all those wonderful ideas that would make America great.

Probably closer to the actual state of affairs, psychologically as well as historically, is Ira Morris' 1900 account of the dark times following the Revolution. "But perhaps no locality in the whole country," Morris writes, "witnessed more material changes among its people at that period than Staten Island." He then goes on to describe the conflict between Islanders of British, French, and Dutch extraction, as well as the wrinkle introduced by British and Hessian deserters.

> Truly the first days of the Republic were dark. A feeling of absolute unrest pervaded every home on the Island. At every turn there were the keenest reminders of war. Desolation marked every locality.... Added to this was a greater cause still for the unrest and dissatisfaction of the people. The bitter feelings engendered by the war found no abatement here when peace spread her white wings over the land.... Tory and Rebel were ready epithets to be applied in the roadside smithy, the village store, aye—at the very church door...Persecution crept into the daily acts of both sides. Neither would forgive anything the other had done....

In subsequent chapters Morris presents an account of Staten Island history in the nineteenth century that gives evidence of an Island whose development mirrors in microcosm many of the stresses, strains and tensions of an urbanizing and industrializing America. Controversy over development of the north shore, Jacksonian-Whig animosities, the building and burning of the Quarantine, Know-Nothingism, and the Civil War draft riots: they all are here, rich evidence of a people fully caught up in the great issues of their day.

Two years ago in *The Staten Island Historian* I published an essay largely critical of the post World War II writers of Staten Island history. Concentrating on Vernon Hampton, Henry Steinmeyer and Dorothy Valentine Smith, I found their work narrowly cast and pietistic. They proffered an interpretation of Staten Island history that held the passage of the past to the present to be virtually conflict-free and benign. The world of Staten Island, as they presented it, was the world of a bucolic village filled with good neighbors. This of course was not absolutely untrue, but it was far from the whole truth. Most of those today who have some understanding of Staten Island history, however, have acquired it from these writers. Unlike the earlier histories of the Island, most of which run into the hundreds if not thousands of pages, the works of these three writers are short and readable in the course of an evening. If only because of this, they become the work of choice for anyone desiring a quick fix on Island history. And in this fashion they render a disservice for they present an overly simplified and distorted version of what Staten Island has been. It is that version of events that has become such a potent force in contemporary politics.

What I have been attempting to make clear is that whether or not secession is a good thing for Staten Island, there is no golden age to which one can return. A close examination of the past will show us that Staten Island has never been isolated from history but that, just like people everywhere, Staten Islanders have always struggled to shape their encounter with it.

Perhaps it is for this reason that I admire so much William T. Davis' *Days Afield on Staten Island*. Davis, the self-educated but world renowned naturalist, published the book when he was thirty, in 1892, and reissued it in 1937. It is a charming little book, a recognized classic, a delight to read, and much easier to get through than the five volume *Staten Island And Its People* he wrote with Charles Leng in the 1920s. What resonates so eloquently in Davis' book is the pained ambivalence with which he looks upon the changes transforming Staten Island. A man who literally knew every tree on the Island and whose trampings were legend and legion for over half-a-century, he felt keenly and intimately the passage of the Island into the City of New York. He heard the whistle of the train in once sylvan fields, crossed pipes bringing petroleum from Pennsylvania, saw the spread of telephones poles, watched open fields give way to suburban development, and lived to see automobiles and street lights transform the night; big government—the building of Borough Hall—literally took away the view of the harbor he had enjoyed for most of his life. But he did not despair. As a naturalist Davis knew that struggle and change were the essential ingredients of life and development. Without them there was only stagnation and death. So as the Island was drawn more directly into the orbit of the City, he acted to preserve its past for future generations. The Staten Island Institute of Arts & Sciences, the Staten Island Historical Society, and the Billopp

Conference House are all legacies of "Bug" Davis, crucial institutions in the preserving and fostering of public memory, without which public identity is shrouded in myth. Yet even Davis was not immune to the lure and magic of the Island's past. The final paragraph of *Days Afield* reads:

> Nature does indeed will us strange fortunes, but generally she is tolerably kind, and if we do not try to visit the North Pole, or spend a Summer in the Sahara, we may live along without any marked break in our mutual, friendly relations. We may go musing calmly in the meadows, in the woodland, and along the country lanes, and back to those inward murmurings of fancy that cause a strange army of natural and human transactions to move in turn over Staten Island, that seems to sleep so peacefully today under the autumn sun. The patroons and the bouweries, the Peach war, the British troops quartered on the Island, and the domestic scenes in the Dutch and Huguenot families, wear to us a garment of quiet and pleasant interest, though its seams chafed harshly enough, many of those who wore it of old. No doubt the present is quite as unquiet and wrangling as many a bygone year, but over the past there always rests a halo, and time, like a kind critic, idealizes for us the jumbled maze, and only gives forth a poetic tincture of the whole.

Left: Cornelius G. Kolff. Right: William T. Davis.

Figure 1. E. Keating/NYT Permissions.

The Island Image: Reflections and Refractions from Home and Abroad

Charles L. Sachs

On Sunday, January 30, 1994, *The New York Times Magazine* featured on its cover a striking color photograph, heralding the magazine's lead article "Escape from New York," an essay on the Staten Island secession movement. The article was written by Chip Brown, a contributing editor of *Esquire*, and illustrated with color photographs (including the cover image) by Edward Keating. The piece represents probably the most prominently placed, and widely disseminated, recent published effort to "profile" and illustrate Staten Island—and its (or, I should say, *our*) community image and identity—for a broad regional and national audience. Appearing at a critical moment in the secession effort—after the overwhelmingly favorable 1993 referendum supporting the draft independent city charter for Staten Island, yet before any further legislative action has been taken in Albany—the article raises questions about the Island's—and Islanders'—public image and self-definition. The pictures, especially, warrant critical examination as contributions to a long, historic visual tradition.[1]

What do these images say about Staten Island and the Island's visual character—as a place, a landscape, a community? Equally important, what do they indicate about an image's *source*? Finally, can we, by looking back through the archival record of Island imagery, discover central themes, perspectives, and traditions of representation that provide insight not only into these recent photographs, but also into historic perceptions and appreciations of Staten Island identity?

At present, I can only suggest—in brief outline—preliminary results of a work in progress—my effort to explore and rediscover historic Staten Island imagery, especially its photography in the 19th and early 20th centuries.[2] I hope this introduction will encourage others to delve further into aspects of this topic.

From the perspective of a student of Staten Island iconography and an Islander, the article in the *New York Times Magazine* is a very *disturbing* piece of illustrated journalism, especially in its presentation and use of photographs. The overriding tone set by the text is cynical, abrasive, condescending. The author apostrophizes: "O, Staten Island!—38,507 acres of incongruity and contradiction where the 'hills' are bedrock and the 'mountains' are garbage, and the official flower is either the pinkster azalea or the escaped plastic bag. Staten Island is the land of Kiwanis Clubs and big gas guzzlers for sale on small front lawns, and guys who don't split the checks with their dates, and girls who wear high heels at the grocery store and marry young." Moreover, the selection and framing of the images are pointedly deceptive.

The ambiguous cover picture [Figure 1]—of cheerless, staid, or angry, and curious white men and children's faces and the faceless woman's body with the "Vote Yes" Staten Island secession button confronting the photojournalist's camera in an undefined landscape at the edge of what might be a parade, political rally, or demonstration—is clearly meant to evoke associations with recent news photos of nationalist movements, especially in the former Soviet Union, the Balkans, and elsewhere along the border regions of Europe and Asia. The conscious symbolism is reinforced by the title, "Separatism Surging," and the caption: "The fires of secession burn among proud, resentful Staten Islanders, just as they do among Azerbaijanis, Kurds, Quebecois—and Californians."

The lead image for the essay [Figure 2]—a two page spread—portrays a common event—a "decisive moment" (to borrow the French photographer Cartier-Bresson's phrase) in the daily lives of thousands of Island commuters—the morning ferry debarkation in Manhattan. Here is a group portrait of the range of Staten Island faces—black and white, men and women—determined, tired, probably anxious to reach their destination—work, school, appointments or interviews, perhaps requiring the additional, trying transfer to subway or bus. The weather is cold and somewhat wet, yet the caption elevates the commuters' poses and expres-

Figure 2. E. Keating/NYT Permissions.

sions to political and cultural parable: "Staten Islanders prepare to step off the ferry for yet another day in 'the city.' They're tired of New York's problems, New York's snobbery. New York."

The pictures of the Island landscape are no less idiosyncratic and allegorical. Three images are particularly noteworthy visual expressions of the article's jaundiced point of view.

A dreary, oddly haunting, lifeless North Shore streetscape [Figure 3] is captioned (sarcastically) "The Bustle": "The No Parking sign is familiar, but not much else about Richmond Terrace seems to say 'New York City.'" Here, the weather could not have been more oppressive. The sky, a nearly colorless gray; the street, vacant of traffic and puddled from a very recent or continuing drizzle. The tree is leafless; the ground, muddy. For anyone who has been on Richmond Terrace—or anywhere in the City—on a cold, wet winter early morning—perhaps a Sunday—the scene is familiar. The distortion represented here is two-fold: First, even the most urbane, prosperous sections of Manhattan and Brooklyn could be made to look as abandoned and depressed as this Staten Island scene when selectively framed at an appropriately empty moment under a cold, gray, wet sky. Second, the commercial streetscape along the port's industrial waterfront represented in this picture, which appears even more raw and desolate under these weather and light conditions, is not unique to Staten Island, but is very much a feature of *Greater* "New York City" and the metropolitan regional landscape. Many similar views can be found in sections of the Bronx, Queens, Brooklyn, and even Manhattan, or for that matter, Perth Amboy, Bayonne, Elizabeth, or Newark. In fact, these *regional* affinities have often been the subject for exploration by illustrators, photographers, and graphic artists during much of this century. The editors of *The WPA Guide to New York City*, for instance, presented a series of artists' renderings of Staten Island as part of a group of prints that included Brooklyn's Columbia Heights and Sheepshead Bay, the Bronx's Westchester Creek, and Queens' Astoria, and Jamaica Bay.[3] The *New York Times Magazine*'s presentation ignores these connections in order to exaggerate a symbolic distinction between Staten Island and the "bustle" of "New York City."

The illustration captioned "Worlds Away: The Manhattan skyline, as seen from New Brighton" [Figure 4] intentionally obscures—through a maze of telephone wires, poles, and municipal street furniture—the spectacular, foreshortened view of the lower Manhattan skyline that emerges

Figure 3. E. Keating/NYT Permissions.

as one passes over the crest of the hill on Victory Boulevard at Silver Lake toward St. George. Not only does the photographer's vantage point denigrate one of the Island's most salient features and historically greatest attractions—its dramatic harbor vistas and picturesque waterfront setting—but the camera frame also avoids portraying any details or suggesting the ambiance of the local streetscape. We are not shown where Staten Islanders live, walk, drive, play, shop, or work. Instead, what is presented here is symbolic, metaphoric "distance." What is especially interesting about this treatment is that it partakes of—but ultimately distorts—a long and dominant tradition of visual representation by painters, printmakers, publishers, and photographers, in which the Island is portrayed as an elevated central feature of an idyllic harbor landscape scene.

By far the most disconcerting (and deceptive) image in the article is the last one included [Figure 5]. Titled "Another View," it is captioned "A Richmondtown man's daily constitutional takes him within smelling distance of the 2,500 acres of city garbage at the Fresh Kills landfill." Here, purportedly, is a south shore residential scene, a landscape view of the Island's historic central village and former county seat. Instead, what is portrayed is a condemned (abandoned but still partly occupied) early

20th-century concrete-block house with shanty outbuildings, along Arthur Kill Road, at the closed Brookfield Landfill site adjoining the Fresh Kills. The dilapidated City-owned site is certainly connected to the historic community concern with municipal garbage dumping and environmental pollution on Staten Island. Yet, as a portrait of a mid-island neighborhood or a representative local resident's daily experience, the image is unrecognizable and false. Like the picture of Richmond Terrace in the rain, this image evokes a spirit of bleakness, cold, and alienation—gray skies, leafless trees, light snow on unkempt ground; a decrepit site; sheet-metal-boarded and vacant, glassless windows; a solitary figure in winter garb. To identify this as Richmondtown, as if it represented anything like the state of existence of even a small percentage of Islanders, or the milieu, landscape, historic character, or architecture of Staten Island is a gross distortion. By misrepresenting the character of this bleak scene, and associating it with the secessionist opposition to the Fresh Kills dump, the article effectively mocks the aesthetic and environmental quality of life on Staten Island.

What *The New York Times Magazine* article does *not* show in its Island portrait is as instructive as what it includes: there are no waterfront scenes (active or de-industrial); no bridges; no historic buildings or sites; no housing; no beaches, parks, or Greenbelt; no shopping centers or Mall; no Navy Home Port or Teleport; no landfill views; no schools, libraries, or government facilities; no South Shore at all. The intent of the article is clearly anti-documentary. Instead, the careful construction and highly selected use of photographs serves as a form of ironic reflection and commentary, an extension of the author's condescending view of Staten Island identity. The overriding impression left by these images is of a dreary, alienated landscape and people. This viewpoint represents a sharp departure from earlier traditions of depicting Staten Island.

About a century and a half before Edward Keating photographed his purported "Richmondtown" view for the *New York Times Magazine*, a twenty-year-old local painter executed a canvas of a landscape scene from a nearby vantage point [Figure 6]. Jasper F. Cropsey's *Cortelyou Farm, Greenridge* (painted in 1843) is also one of the oldest known Staten Island landscape and residential scenes. Preserved in the Staten Island Historical Society (SIHS) Collection, it is one of the earliest surviving works by the Staten Island-born artist and architect (1823-1900), who is best known for his dramatic landscape paintings of the Hudson

Figure 4. E. Keating/NYT Permissions.

River School. The canvas depicts the 80-acre farmstead owned by a relative of the artist, and one of his first patrons, Lawrence H. Cortelyou. The property, with its two farmhouses, located along Arthur Kill Road in the valley along the Fresh Kills approximately one mile west of Richmondtown, remained in the Cortelyou family until the turn of the 20th century, when it was purchased by a real estate firm for prospective subdivision and development. The site today is occupied by the "Atrium" shopping center and movie theater complex.

Cropsey's canvas portrays an image of rural pride, prosperity, and order, far from the crowded, dirty, and dangerous metropolis across the Bay. Richmondtown, a neat country village, and the tidal mill and farmsteads along the Fresh Kills, glow in the middle distance. This work in many ways epitomizes the rural-romantic vision of the Island, which dominated much of the imagery produced in the 19th and early 20th centuries.

From the first European contacts with the people and landscape of the Hudson River Basin to the late 18th-century, graphic images of Staten Island were largely restricted to navigational charts, maps, land surveys, and extremely rare distant landscape renderings. This topographical ("plan and prospect") tradition applied equally, during this period, to European depictions of most New World localities, including urban centers, such as Manhattan.[4] Archibald Robertson's famous watercolor drawing "View of the Narrows between Long Island and Staten Island with our Fleet at Anchor and Lord Howe coming in / Taken from the heights above the Watering Place Staten Island, 12th July, 1776," in the New York Public Library's Spenser Collection, is probably the only detailed, contemporary depiction of a Staten Island scene extant from before the mid-1830s, when Island views began appearing regularly as popular subjects for commercial printmakers and landscape painters.[5] By the 1840s and 1850s, the Island also began to attract the attention of experimental photographers.

The popular image of Staten Island that emerged in the 1830s, and remained the dominant icon at least through the end of the century, presented the Island as a picturesque setting, a retreat and haven from the big city woes and unpleasantness of Manhattan. According to this view, Staten Island appears bucolic, an attractive natural area, pleasingly modified—tilled and tamed—by man, a key element within a dramatic—romantic yet placid—harborscape, which connects, as well as separates it from the City core. Dozens, if not hundreds, of examples of this type of

Figure 5. E. Keating/NYT Permissions.

Figure 6.

image were produced in a variety of media, and published and exhibited, from the 1830s (beginning with the aquatints of William James Bennett, the engravings of William Henry Bartlett's *American Scenery*—published in London—and early lithographs by Nathaniel Currier) through the turn of the 20th century.

Among the many noteworthy examples from the 1830s is "New Brighton from New York Bay" from *Richmond County Mirror*, volume 1 (July 1837), engraved by John A. Rolph (1799-1862) after a painting by John Gadsby Chapman (1808-1889) [Figure 7].[6] This engraving, inset as a frontispiece to the first issue of a Staten Island-printed newspaper, presents and promotes the Island as an idyllic suburban retreat. Note the sloops, schooners, rowboats, and wildfowl in the Bay and Kill; a diminutive, rather innocuous, steam ferry at the dock at the foot of York Avenue, and the "Greek temples" of Richmond Terrace, the Pavilion Hotel, and the single (recently opened) building at Sailors' Snug Harbor.

The development of this type of image coincided with a period of extraordinary economic and social change, affiliated with the rapid commercial, industrial, and demographic growth of Manhattan. From the 1810s, the Island attracted many of the city's business elite seeking real estate investments, residences, and summer retreats away from the dangers and discomforts of Manhattan—especially after the yellow fever and cholera epidemics of the 1820s-1830s and the Great Fire of 1835. By the 1830s, the Island was in the middle of a suburban and institutional building boom: a suburb and hotel resort was founded at New Brighton (1834-35), and other developments included Stapleton (1833-34), Elliotville (1836), Clifton (1837), Rossville (1837), and Port Richmond (c.1838). The Island also became the setting for institutions, particularly maritime philanthropies and health care facilities: Sailor's Snug Harbor (1831-33) and Seamen's Retreat (Clifton, 1834-37) constructed monumental complexes; Mariners Family Home (Stapleton, 1854) and the Society for Seamen's Children (Port Richmond, 1849) were more modest in concept and design. This influx of population, which concentrated on the north and eastern shores, was so intense that dividing lines between developments blurred: by 1840, the area appeared to many observers as "almost a continued village."

Other wealthy New Yorkers and Yankee expatriates (such as the young Frederick Law Olmsted) obtained southshore holdings to work experimentally as gentlemen-farmers. Many of these newcomers—such as Samuel Akerly, Olmsted, the Anthons, and others—were among the first to document the island's geology, ecology, agriculture, history, and folklore. It should not be surprising, therefore, that the dominant graphic image promulgated of and for the island during this seminal period was romantic, rural, and picturesque. "The whole island is like a garden, and affords very fine scenery," noted Henry David Thoreau during a visit to the home of Judge William Emerson, on Emerson Hill, in 1843. "God might have made a more beautiful place than Staten Island, but He didn't," wrote the prominent man-of-letters George William Curtis later in the century.

This icon remains powerful today, as seen in the following examples from the 1850s and later. "The Narrows from Staten Island, New York" [Figure 8] is a wood engraving (with added hand coloring), drawn by W. R. Miller and published in *Gleason's Pictorial*, October 1, 1853. The view was drawn from Pavilion Hill; part of Tompkinsville and the old Planters Hotel are visible in the foreground, while New York Bay, Stapleton, Clifton, Fort Wadsworth, and the Narrows form the background; the Seamen's Retreat can be seen at Clifton. Here is Staten Island as the summer retreat and picnic ground for city dwellers.[7]

Advances in printing technology enabled high-speed mass-production of wood-engraved illustrations, and fostered the rise of popular weekly illustrated news magazines. *Gleason's Pictorial Drawing Room Companion*, issued in Boston beginning in 1851, was soon overshadowed by the major New York competitors: *Frank Leslie's Illustrated Weekly Newspaper* (1855), which within five years attained a national readership of over 160,000 per issue, and *Harper's Weekly* (1857), which under editor (and Staten Island resident) George William Curtis, reached a circulation of 120,000. The illustrated weeklies' wood engravings document scenes, events, and people, many of which escaped the attention of more academic artists or early photographers. The pictures were geared to a mass, largely middle-class audience.

"View from New Brighton, Staten Island, on the Narrows, N.Y." [Figure 9] is also from *Gleason's Pictorial*, September 30, 1854. The wood engraving, hand colored, was drawn from Fort Hill and depicts an ironically healthful-looking outdoor recreational view of horseback riders outside the gates of the Quarantine hospital grounds.[8]

These romantic graphic conventions were, on occasion, subject to subtle variations, particularly after the Civil War, in the 1870s and 1880s,

Figure 7.

Figure 8.

Figure 9.

Figure 10.

Figure 11.

when features of the industrial landscape were sometimes incorporated into picturesque harborscape scenes. In "New York Bay from the Narrows" [Figure 10], a steel engraving, by F. B. Schell and E. H. Smith, issued c.1880, wealthy promenaders and picnickers are shown enjoying the outdoors and spectacular harbor views above Ft. Wadsworth; while in the distance are ominous clouds and factory smoke of the city (west side Manhattan) and nearby industrial centers (New Jersey and the north shore of Staten Island).

Mid-19th-century artistic renderings of Staten Island's "character" were, in rare instances, not restricted to landscape and topographic views. One of the most evocative—amusing and effective—attempts to portray a prominent species of new Island resident through the genre of the humorous, theatrical urban "street type." In this Sheet Music cover, "The Staten Island Gentleman, Comic Ballade, Words by Champion Bissell" [Figure 11], music by Thomas Baker, published by Firth, Pond & Co., 547 Broadway; lithograph by Sarony, Major & Knapp, 449 Broadway, 1859, the image reflects the trials and tribulations of the harried Staten Island suburban ferry commuter, late 1850s-style. A lower Manhattan merchant or businessman, responsible for household marketing on his way home, dashes frantically to catch the ferry, dropping a package in the process.[9]

By the late 1840s and early 1850s, an alternative graphic approach and subject matter had also clearly begun to emerge on (and for) the Island. Less familiar today than the romantic, picturesque landscape, this imagery emphasized—documented and promoted—industrial and commercial development. Driven by the rapid expansion and visible prominence of manufacturing, building construction, and commerce throughout the metropolitan region, these images—at first engravings, then lithographs, photographs, and halftone renditions—presented factories, shops, stores, offices, workers, and products as proud emblems of modern industrial progress. Many of these images served to advertise and celebrate the businesses and products shown.

The engraved view of "The New-York Dyeing and Printing Establishment" [Figure 12] (SIHS) was printed on one side of an advertising handbill (Lossing-Barritt, N.Y., engravers; Oliver & Brothers, printers, NYC), about 1856. The print depicts Staten Island's first major industrial plant and one of its longest-lived industries, which was established in 1819 in West New Brighton, then named Factoryville (for its novelty); the works closed during the Great Depression. Note how the emissions from the smokestacks are so boldly rendered, with evident pride. The same image was published in a promotional feature article in the *Staten Islander* newspaper, February 16, 1856.

By the 1860s, some commercial artists and illustrators also began to experiment with ways to mediate or meld the rural-romantic and commercial-industrial icons. One of the most striking examples of this trend is illustrated in the "Fresh from the Farm" [Figure 13] Staten Island Preserving House, Long Neck, label for produce crate or can, c. 1865 (SIHS), in which the brightly-colored, bountiful agricultural scene features men and women field laborers, heavy horse-drawn wagons, and the monumental canning factory replete with smoking stack and prominent American flag.

The 1840s and 1850s brought the prospect of a new mechanical form of representation, photography, to Staten Island image-making. The earliest known photographs made of or on Staten Island date from about 1859, two decades after the introduction of the first practical photographic process—the daguerreotype—to New York (and America) in 1839. No daguerrian studios are known to have been established here, but several pioneering figures in the history of the medium—Dr. John William Draper and Howard J. Chilton—have local associations. The legendary Matthew Brady lived on Staten Island, probably on Grymes Hill, intermittently during the period before the Civil War, when he was operating his daguerrian (later photographic) gallery in Manhattan.

Figure 12.

Unfortunately, no Brady local views—if indeed he did photograph here—have as yet been discovered.

It was not until August 1859 that a commercial photographic business advertised on Staten Island. Very little is known about H. Hoyer (his first name has not been discovered), a man who suddenly arrived and then almost immediately departed from the community by May 1860. About two dozen different Hoyer stereocards, "American Views," all dating from around 1859 and all depicting local scenes, landmarks, and buildings, predominantly in the Tompkinsville-Clifton area, survive in the Staten Island Historical Society and Staten Island Institute of Arts and Sciences (SIIAS) collections. These photographs—clearly focused, simple, somewhat crude, and less than artfully framed—represent an important departure in Staten Island imagery. Hoyer, like many outdoor commercial photographers of the period, practiced a straightforward documentary approach, and much of the appeal of his work—as well as that of his successors in this tradition—is due to the unembellished, mechanically "factual" impression this produced, as seen in the following examples of his work: H. Hoyer, St. Mary's Church, Bay Street, Clifton, c.1859, half-stereo (SIHS) [Figure 14] and H. Hoyer, Ruins of the Quarantine, 1859, half-stereo (SIHS) [Figure 15], in which he captured the almost classical ruins of the State Quarantine Station in

Figure 13.

60 Community, Continuity and Change

Figure 14.

Figure 15.

62 Community, Continuity and Change

Figure 16.

Figure 17.

Tompkinsville, about a year after the smoke from the incendiary protest of September 1, 1858 had cleared.

The late 19th-century and early 20th-century photographic images that survive of Staten Island are richly varied in format, subject matter, and approach or perspective, ranging from the stylized formal landscape and studio portrait to the casual snapshot document. There were more than twenty commercial photographers operating businesses on Staten Island prior to 1900, all of which were located in the northern and eastern shore village centers or resort areas. At least six of these photographers—John Loeffler, August Loeffler, George Michel, John Lake, Isaac Almstaedt, and George Bear—produced noteworthy work, at times embracing all three major iconographic traditions: the picturesque, industrial/commercial, and documentary traditions. Here one example will have to suffice: a cabinet card photograph by Isaac Almstaedt of the Staten Island Athletic Club Boathouse, Richmond Terrace, New Brighton, c.1885 (SIHS) [Figure 16].

Independent itinerants (most unidentified today) and representatives of New York, Brooklyn, and New Jersey-based studios, also travelled the roads of Staten Island to solicit clients for landscape views, house and shop portraits. The makers of few of the extremely limited number of surviving outdoor ambrotype and tintype views of the Island, such as [Figure 17], an extraordinary tintype of the family, coach, and coachman at the Latourette House, Richmond (now Golf Clubhouse), c.1870 (original in SIIAS), are known. And a remarkable document of a mid-island disastrous event: the ruins of Church of St. Andrew, Richmondtown after fire, c.1867–68 (SIHS) [Figure 18].

By the late 1860s, these professionals were joined by at least one serious, talented amateur, John Jeremy Crooke (1824–1911), a civil and mining engineer, inventor, and naturalist. Crooke purchased extensive land holdings in the area of Great Kills or Giffords, including the peninsula that bears his name (Crooke's Point), between 1857 and 1866, where he established a home for his family. Approximately 120 of Crooke's original collodion-on-glass negatives, which date from c. 1866 to 1871, survive today, as do about an equal number of his vintage albumen prints, in the SIIAS. Although limited by the early "wet plate" (or collodion emulsion) technology to extremely slow exposures and the need for immediate development of the negatives, Crooke succeeded in capturing a broad range of subject matter and of achieving some startling artistic

64   *Community, Continuity and Change*

Figure 18.

Figure 19.

effects. He worked both indoors and out. He experimented with dramatic studio lighting (and created a series of remarkable family portraits). He posed theatrical tableaux genre scenes; captured people (carpenters, farmers, fishermen) poised in mid-task; made humorous portraits, including family pets; produced picturesque land- and sea-scapes, as well as more matter-of-fact record views of the natural and built environment—houses and sheds, furnished room interiors, boats, machinery and engines, and a steam locomotive, for example. "Women and Child" [Figure 19], a modern contact print made from a J. J. Crooke sterograph, displays Crooke family members examining a photograph album on the porch of "Liberty Hall," c.1866–71 (SIIAS).

While obviously more staged and static in appearance than the freer, faster dry-plate era pictures that would follow in the 1880s and 1890s, Crooke's photographs have a strong visual appeal and provide a rare varied glimpse inside late-1860s Staten Island. As such, they serve as prelude to the wide range of styles and diverse subjects adopted by Staten Island photographers—both amateurs and professionals—from the 1880s. Figures 20-22 are a small, random sample of Island photographs drawn from the SIHS collection.[10]

As the diversity of these images suggests—contrary to the impression fostered by the author and photographer of the *New York Times Magazine*'s "Escape from New York"—Staten Island has been a far more richly varied place than is generally comprehended or appreciated. Anyone who lives or has lived here, or bothers to look around the borough, knows that Staten Island is—and has always been—a place of remarkable internal contrasts and changes. By acknowledging and, indeed, seeking out and exploring the Island's exceptionally fertile visual history—we can reclaim and preserve the Island's past and help fashion new images for the future. Whether or not Staten Island ever finally secedes from New York City, it is important to recognize that the Island's culture, social life, economy, and self-image have been created and refined through a process of continuous influx of new visitors and residents. In fact, it is largely due to a long history of invasion and adoption of the Island by steady streams of what the farmers in the 1830s called "forners" (the majority of whom came from New York and other boroughs of the Greater City), that the traditional images of the island were created and the island's history recorded. There has been a continuous interplay among the island, the greater port district, and the central

Figure 20. Aerial photographer unknown, McWilliams Shipyard fire, West New Brighton waterfront, 1947.

Top: Figure 21. Charles A. Meyer collection: Arthur Schoefse and William Holliday boxing, Feb. 10, 1901. *Bottom:* Figure 22. Brassington Family Collection: Parlor group with men dressed as women, c.1905.

cities' business districts (Manhattan and Brooklyn) of the metropolis. Despite our literal *insularity* (or geographic separateness), one cannot understand—or portray—Staten Island in isolation from Manhattan, the metropolitan/port district, or the greater Hudson Basin harbor region of which it has always been an integral part.

Notes

1. Chip Brown, "Escape from New York," *The New York Times Magazine* (January 30, 1994), 20-25,42-44,50,60.
2. This paper draws upon and supplements research presented in Charles L. Sachs, "Alice Austen's Predecessors and Contemporaries: Photography on Staten Island in the 19th and Early 20th Centuries," *Staten Island Historian*: n.s.11: 1 (Summer-Fall 1993), 1-16.
3. *The WPA Guide to New York City* (New York: Random House, 1939; repr., New York: Pantheon Books, 1982). See plates, between pp. 540-541, with prints by Minetta Good, Louis Lozowick, David Burke, Harry Leroy Taskey, Anne Nooney, and Mabel Dwight.
4. See, especially, John Kouwenhoven's incomparable *The Columbia Historical Portrait of New York* (Garden City, New York: Doubleday & Company, 1953), 107; also, Hugh Powell, "Historic Prints of Staten Island, 1763-1876," *Proceedings of the Staten Island Institute of Arts and Sciences* 34:2 (Fall 1989): 91-222.
5. Kouwenhoven, 73.
6. See Powell, "Historic Prints of Staten Island," 112-13.
7. See Powell, 141.
8. See Powell, 142-43. New York State established a Quarantine hospital station—for isolating ship passengers, immigrants, and seamen entering the Port of New York who were diseased or suspected of carrying contagious illness—on the northeastern shore of Staten Island (the area later named Tompkinsville) in 1799. Although the thirty-acre site, according to one 19th century reminiscence, "looked very beautiful from the water, having some fine trees, well kept lawns and gardens and fairly good looking buildings," the Quarantine was also feared and reviled by the majority of Staten Islanders as "a pestiferous local nuisance, and a constant menace to the

health of New York City and the whole surrounding country." In 1857 and 1858, Staten Islanders joined together to oppose the expansion of Quarantine station; when a series of public protests were ignored, a group of prominent citizens carefully removed all patients and burned the facility to the ground on the evenings of September 1 and 2, 1858. The station was eventually transferred to an offshore floating hospital and then to Hoffman and Swinburne islands. See Dr. F. Hollick, "The Old Quarantine. Its Destruction and the Causes Which Led to It." *Proceedings of the Natural Science Association of Staten Island*, Special No. 16 (October 1893): pp. 64-67.

9. See Powell, 158-59.
10. I have concentrated in this paper on the work of local photographers who are less familiar to contemporary audiences. This approach naturally neglects E. Alice Austen (1866-1952), a talented and energetic amateur documentary photographer, whose historic Rosebank home, "Clear Comfort," is both a New York City Landmark and National Historic Landmark. In part through the efforts of preservationists and social historians since the 1950s, Ms. Austen is today Staten Island's most famous photographer. The majority of Austen's surviving negatives—as well as a significant collection of the photographer's vintage prints and documents—are preserved in the SIHS collection. The largest published selection of Austen images—as well as the best biographical study currently available—remains Ann Novotny's *Alice's World, The Life and Photography of an American Original: Alice Austen, 1866-1952* (Old Greenwich, CT: The Chatham Press, 1976). Austen's work uses an assortment of styles to address a broad range of subject matter—at times romantic, pastoral, picturesque (as in her sumptuous views of the Clear Comfort landscape, porch, parlors, and lawn); starkly documentary and straightforward (as in her raw depictions of Quarantine laboratories and fumigation facilities on Hoffman and Swinburne Islands); or comically playful and intimate (as in her costumed masquerade portraits of female friends in male attire).

Twice Upon an Island Revisited: Another Look at Staten Island's Role in the Landscapes and Planning of Frederick Law Olmsted

Howard R. Weiner

In 1968 Bradford M. Greene, writing in the *Proceedings of the S. I. Institute of Arts and Sciences,* described how America's foremost park planner Frederick Law Olmsted twice chose Staten Island as his home.[1] It is the intention of this paper to explore the part Staten Island played in the metamorphosis of Olmsted into an urban planner and his suggestions for the development of the Island. Finally, some of the literature exploring the reasons for Olmsted's changing vision will be examined.

"There's been a burst of rediscovery," writes Tony Hiss, author of a forthcoming book about Olmsted. "We're just starting to come to terms with his legacy. So I want to look at how his works affect the lives of Americans today!"[2] Best known as the nineteenth century planner of Central Park, Prospect Park, and the Boston Park system and numerous other landscapes, Olmsted is now embraced by all sorts of environmentalists, regional planners, recreation experts and students of democratic urban life.[3] Mike Davis, a leading chronicler of the anguished recent history of Los Angeles, writes of the end of the Olmstedian vision of public space with its conceptions of public landscapes and parks as social safety valves and places for the mixing of classes and ethnicities while experiencing recreation and pleasure. Davis quotes Olmsted's statement that "No one who has closely observed the conduct of the people who visit (Central) Park can doubt that it exercises a distinctly harmonizing and refining influence upon the most lawless classes of the city—an influence favorable to courtesy, self control and temperance."[4]

Olmsted's Staten Island experience helps us to understand how seemingly natural landscapes are, in fact, elaborate constructs of art, engineering and social theory.[5] His Staten Island farm gave Olmsted both the intellectual and physical materials with which to work out these schemes. Here, Olmsted planned the integration of the rural, urban, scientific, moral and transcendental ingredients of nineteenth century life. A study of this process may help explain his agonizing confrontation with the great metropolis.

Olmsted was born in Hartford Connecticut in 1822 and experienced small town puritan New England. His mother died when he was young. He spent much time walking and riding with his family through picturesque landscapes. He was boarded out to several ministers and was expected to attend Yale, as might be expected of the son of a prosperous merchant. An eye disorder brought on by sumac poisoning led to only informal attendance at Yale and tutoring in typographical engineering. An unhappy experience as a dry goods clerk ended in his choice of farming as a career. Wanderlust led to nine months as a crew member at sea before his father bought him a farm at Guilford, Connecticut in 1847. From the beginning he sought to become a scientific farmer as well as country squire. But his notion of squire was that of an educator and cultivator of the intellect of the producing class. His Connecticut farm proved too small and unproductive for such ambitious goals. Through family connections it was arranged in 1848 for Olmsted to have the Arkerly farm in the Arden Woods section of Staten Island.[6]

Olmsted stated upon taking up scientific farming on Staten Island that "I want to make myself useful in the world—to make happy—to help advance the condition of society and hasten the preparation for the millennium. . . ."[7] To his friend Charles Loring Brace, he had implored in 1847 "Throw your light on the path in Politics and Social Improvement and encourage me to put foot down and forward. There's a great work that wants doing in this our generation, Charley, lets off our jacket and go about it."[8]

The period 1815-1860 was the "Farmer's Age." Scientific farming was a response to the growth in demand for agricultural products by an increasingly urban society. Referring to his Staten Island experience, Olmsted felt he was a good farmer and a good neighbor. He served on the school committee, improved the highways and was secretary of the local farmer's club and the County Agricultural Society, took prizes for the best wheat and turnips and best assortment of fruit, imported an English machine and, in partnership with a friend, established the first drainage tile works in America.[9]

The Arkerly place had extensive and varied acreage with a sea view. One area was a high plateau with red clay, good for growing grain. The farm house was an old stone structure with extensive porches. Ships were visible coming and going from the docks of Manhattan. Olmsted brought equipment from his Connecticut farm to the newly named "Southside." He had a sloop loaded with animals, plants and furniture. The new Staten Islander began to feel at home when he was well received by his neighbors of Dutch and Huguenot descent who served a dinner and spoke about their farming experiences and the future of Staten Island. A friendly circle developed around Olmsted, his brother John, Charles Loring Brace and the family of Dr. Cyrus Perkins, a former Dartmouth surgery professor. Olmsted honed his conversational skills and made use of Perkins' library.[10]

Perkins' granddaughter, Mary, who later married John Olmsted, described Olmsted in his early days on Staten Island: "Frederick was at this time 26 years of age, full of life and fun. He threw himself into farming with enthusiasm, introduced system and order to his men, expecting for one thing that at knocking off time every tool used should be returned to its appointed place and that every chore should be done at the hour fixed; the foremen to report progress before going in to supp."[11] Olmsted laid out fields for wheat, priced potatoes, planned a dock and remodeled the shape of land. He moved a barn because it was in an unattractive sightline. He turfed grasses around the edge of a pond which had looked like a mudhole. Olmsted fenced grazing lands and planted trees.[12]

On Saturday evenings and Sundays brother John, a medical student, and Charles, the future theologian, spoke of their experiences with the ill and poor in the hospitals, prisons and streets of the city. It is important to note that Olmsted's social conscience was developing at the same time he was reordering the land. Here we see Staten Island as a precursor of the amelioratory park. The Olmsteds and Brace were of the Emerson-Lowell generation, which applied moral principles to such issues as abolition, immigration and poverty. While subject to Brace's increasing religiosity, the Olmsteds tended to work their principles into daily routines rather than into any formal worship.[13]

With the coming of the spring 1849, Frederick showed off his emerald green wheat between the house and the sea. He argued over the price of his cabbages. He attended a meeting of fruit growers. It was at this time that his agricultural society work expanded. He supported the building of a new school after his appointment as a trustee. He wrote a letter to the *Staten Islander* about the need for a new plank road. He became knowledgeable about land values and Staten Island's reputation for malaria.

Olmsted became an established member of Staten Island's elite. Olmsted's circle expanded to include Judge Emerson, the brother of Ralph Waldo. Articles about his experience on the Island brought him into correspondence with such men as William Cullen Bryant, Andrew Jackson Downing and other literary and social figures in New York City.

At the same time he attended to his building, land, workers and neighborhood visits. Olmsted's continuing articles on scientific farming led to a career as a journalist. Gradually, the moral principles of amelioration became wedded to his aesthetic and social concerns about the city.

Olmsted lived on Staten Island until 1854. During and after these years, he became a traveler with several of his accounts published in the *New York Times*. He entered into a publishing partnership with George William Curtis which took over *Putnam's Magazine*.[14]

Through Downing, Olmsted met Calvert Vaux with whom he designed and constructed Central Park. When the Civil War commenced he led the Sanitary Commission, the forerunner of the Red Cross. Later he worked on major estates and parks in California. Now a national figure, he accepted an offer of collaboration with Vaux for design and construction of Prospect Park.

In early 1866 he returned to Staten Island, where he was to reside until 1872. Olmsted moved to a house on Amos (now Norwood) St. in Clifton near Vanderbilt's Landing and the ferry to Brooklyn. As a returning figure of stature, Olmsted was prevailed upon by Staten Islands's elite to work on improvements for various properties. It is thought that he was responsible for the wall and gates of the present Notre Dame Academy (then the John J. Cisco Estate). Olmsted laid out the ground of the Mason Estate in Rossville and helped with the planning of Hamilton Park in New Brighton. He befriended the architect Henry H. Richardson who lived nearby in Clifton and the two would work together on many projects. Olmsted also made the acquaintance of William H. Vanderbilt for whom he would build the Vanderbilt family tomb in Staten Island's Moravian Cemetery.[15]

Despite these projects, Olmsted continued to develop more comprehensive views of urban planning. In early 1870 he addressed the American Social Science Association on "Public Parks and the Enlargement of Towns." A major park, argued Olmsted, could be the center of a town from which could spread lines of communication. These ideas led to his conception of planned suburbs such as Riverside, Illinois, a full generation before the Garden City movement. Olmsted's widened horizons and connections with local notables led to an offer to direct the survey of the Staten Island Improvement Commission of 1870. This endeavor would rank with scientific farming experience as Olmsted's two major Staten Island connections.[16]

In 1870 concerned citizens of Staten Island called upon the New York State Legislature to create the Staten Island Improvement Commission. Olmsted wrote a letter to the *New York World* in which he claimed that the Island had failed to grow because its well meaning citizens had remained ignorant of and incompetent for the task at hand. He called for professional help and offered to serve. Richardson and public health expert Dr. Eisha Harris were appointed to serve on the commission directed by Olmsted.[17]

The "Preliminary Scheme of Improvements" was issued in 1871. According to Bradford M. Greene, it was "remarkable in its foresight, good taste and practibility." If the recommendations had been followed Staten Island would today be one of the most beautiful, desirable and convenient places to live in the New York City area. It presented the choices for land development, transportation links, business specialization, and population concentration. It surveyed the dock possibilities, lot sizes, suburban tendencies and drainage needs of the Island. It laid out all sorts of possibilities of aesthetic and practical improvement. A long section dealt with the Island's "undeserved reputation for unhealthfulness." Much of this part dealt with drainage, a continuing problem on Staten Island.[18]

The Report emphasized the need for providing a large number of sites for dwellings to be served by urban public conveniences. It generally described the advantages of landscaping and sylvan beauty. The writers of the 1871 Report predicted a motor age with bridges and highways. The warnings about overdevelopment, small lot size, obstructed views and the need to protect the lands later known as the Greenbelt were precursors of later issues.[19]

Complaints and criticisms by opponents of spending, road building and interference with individual rights poured forth, and most of the report's suggestions were not enacted. Today the 1871 Report appears in urban history texts as an example of intelligent land use. For our purposes it demonstrates how far Olmsted's vision had advanced from his early days of scientific farming.[20]

Bradford M. Greene's quotation from the Report is apt:

> Nowhere on Staten Island is there a landscape or even a glimpse of agreeable scenery which belongs permanently to the public—which no man has the right to obstruct and destroy in pursuance of private and selfish ends. . . . We submit that the Island cannot afford to run the risk of losing this opportunity. . . . We propose no constructed interior roads . . . the character aimed at being that of a rural common. . . . Regarded as a park scheme, much of the glade is already very charmingly planted, the western landscape as seen from all parts of the manor dale [Ocean Terrace at Manor Road] has great breadth and beauty, while from Dongan Knoll [Todt Hill] which is the central feature of the system, the views . . . would be really magnificent, comprehending a grand sweep of the horizon in blue water on one side, in blue hills on the other.

The reasons for this evolution from farmer to park planner are the subject of much analysis. George L. Scheper places Olmsted's metamorphosis in the trend toward nature, moral influence and liberal Protestant reform in the softened religiosity of the romantic-transcendental period. British medieval, manorial and modern aesthetics all required a reworking of the landscape. Proper character formation and collective human happiness were to grow out of the establishment of harmony with nature. Park-like settings figure into a variety of interpretations involving psychology and social engineering. Wordsworth wrote of nature's decisive effect on human character. Life and language would soften in such an environment. Thoreau's accounts of wilderness walks held out the hope of intellectual and physical betterment. British landscaper William Gilpen, and the Swiss physician J. P. von Zimmerman, whose works Olmsted embraced, recommended rural retreats as a corrective to the conditions of urban life. This vision of nature ran counter to the Puritan and frontier call for the subjugation of nature. To some, it is seen as a feminine counterpart of moral influence, inclusion and democracy to the male vision of conquest and domination of the earth. One psychohistorical perspective holds that Olmsted may have used nature as a replacement for his long deceased mother as a counter balance to his powerful father. In any event, service through the influence and refinement of feminine virtues appears to be an important way to view the civilizing influence of Olmsted's parks. Olmsted, whose career developed in the atmosphere of the great mid-century Irish migration and the Draft Riots of 1863 wrote of tempering the behavior of young working class males with a female-based park ethos.[21]

Another postulation is that Olmsted's park could lead a society from an individualistic *Gesellschaft* mentality to a communitarian *Gemeinschaft* ideal. The opposition to Olmsted's work often included the practical men and corrupt politicians of the time.[22]

For biographer Albert Fein, Olmsted's evolution followed major trends in American history. When Olmsted was born America was a predominately agrarian nation. The plan for Central Park was the transitional idea of an ambivalently urban New York City elite. It was motivated by both a tempered Protestantism and the somewhat anti-urban ideas of utopian socialism. By the 1860s the city became more acceptable as an arena of creativity and democracy. As a permanent part of the scene, the city brought forth advocates of environmental planning. The frontier surpassed the city as a threat to civilization. According to Fein, Olmsted's early Staten Island experience, walking tours through Britain and Western Europe, the polarization of the anti-slavery crusade and his editorial experience, all contributed to his acceptance of a more complex urban society. By the time he returned to Staten Island, his parks had become jumping off points for the design of prototypical improved urban environments. By the time of the 1870 Commission, he saw centralized government activity, education of the populace and modern communication as normal urban activities.[23]

In Irving Fisher's biography, morality and place figure large in Olmsted's development. For this Yankee, the small town grouping of buildings around a common with a church, town hall and school made a powerful impression. His family gave him a love of nature but its enjoyment could only be achieved with the addition of moral and utilitarian human effort. His progression toward a farming career occurred during a period of great scientific experimentation in Europe and America and the expansion of Agricultural Societies and journals. His two stays on Staten Island represented the syncretism of these tendencies. The achievement of a satisfactory urban life with the preservation of the environment is a dilemma which still faces the Island.[24]

Roger Starr elaborates on the moral scientific hypothesis by emphasizing the fear of contagious diseases and riots which preoccupied reformist and religious writers. High technology, particularly in sanitary engineering and water supply improvement, was increasing life expectancy. Paradoxically, this technology would arise in the very city where the problems had occurred. Moral regeneration could come from sunlight, relief from the gasses of crowding (later identified as CO), physical exercise and agreeable stimulation of the senses by nature.[25]

Thomas Bender contrasts Olmsted's vision with that of Andrew Jackson Downing. The latter's interest remained with rural structures in their natural setting. His Jeffersonian vision precluded a direct confrontation with the cityscape. Downing shared Olmsted's desire for a less individualistic and disorderly society. But by the time of his second Staten Island experience, Olmsted, the country squire, had become a nineteenth century urban man. There could be no doubt, he wrote in 1870, that all modern civilization involved a strong drift townward. It was more rational to prepare for the continued move to the city than to count upon its subsidence. In fact, he argued the growth of towns was connected to the death of slavery, the end of feudal customs, reduction in overbearing religion and the softening of authoritarian government. He saw the rise of books, newspapers, schools, improved communication and transportation and labor saving devices as connected with the rise of towns. Bender argues that Olmsted's vision with its lingering elitism and sentimentality ran headlong into the Progressive transformation of concern with the "city efficient."[26] Many of Olmsted's ideas found a more democratic expression in the Progressivism of such reformers as Jane Addams. Whether Olmsted's vision is as useful today as Tony Hiss and Mike Davis contend or is important in a mostly nineteenth century context, the two Staten Island periods represent a special view of one man's voyage in the main currents of his time.[27]

Notes

1. Greene, "The Staten Island Improvement Commission of 1870" (part two) *Proc. Of S.I. Institute of Arts and Sciences* March 30, 1968 p. 3.
2. Quoted in Michael Leccese, "News" *Landscape Architecture* (Jan '95) p. 9.
3. Leccese, "News" p. 9.
4. Davis, "Fortress Los Angeles" in Phillip Kasinitz ed., *Metropolis* (N.Y.: NYU Press, 1995) p. 357.
5. Scheper, "The Reformist Vision of F. L. Olmsted and the Poetics of Park Design," *New England Quarterly* (Mar.-Dec. 1989) p. 370.
6. Greene, "Improvement Commission" p. 3-4; Irving D. Fisher *Frederick Law Olmsted and the City Planning Movement in the United States* (Ann Arbor: UMI Research Press,1986) pp. 7-10.
7. Scheper, *Reformist Vision* p. 382.
8. Scheper, *Reformist Vision* p. 382.
9. Scheper, *Reformist Vision* pp. 10-11; Laura Roper *FLO* (Baltimore: Johns Hopkins University Press, 1973) pp. 56-61; Elizabeth Stevenson *Park Maker* (NY: Macmillan, 1977) pp. 42-52.
10. Roper, *FLO* pp. 56-61; Stevenson *Park Maker* 42-52
11. Stevenson, *Park Maker* p. 44.
12. Roper, *FLO* pp. 56-61; Stevenson, *Park Maker* pp. 42-52
13. Starr, "The Motive Behind Olmsted's Park," *The Public Interest* (Winter 84) p. 68. Scheper, "Reformist Vision," pp. 366-378.
14. Greene, "Improvement Commission" pp. 6-8 Roper *FLO*, pp.57-60; Stevenson "Park Maker" pp. 42-57
15. Greene, "Improvement Commission" pp. 6-9
16. White, "Frederick Law Olmsted, the Placemaker" in Daniel Shaffer, ed,. *Two Centuries of American Planning* (Baltimore: John Hopkins University Press, 1988) pp. 97-98
17. Roper, *FLO* pp. 329-362; Greene, "Improvement Commission" pp. 10-19; Albert Fein, *Landscape into Cityscape* (NY: Van Nostrand, 1981), introduction and chapter 5 18. Greene, "Improvement Commission" pp. 10-15
19. Greene, "Improvement Commission" pp. 10-13
20. Greene, "Improvement Commission" p. 15
21. Scheper, "Reformist Vision," pp. 374-378

22. Fisher, *Olmsted*; p. 97.
23. Fein, *Landscape,* introduction; *F. L. Olmsted and the American Environmental Tradition* (NY: Braziller, 1972) pp. 5-27
24. Fisher, *Olmsted*; chaps 2-5
25. Starr, *Motive*, pp. 66-76
26. Bender, *Toward An Urban Vision* (Baltimore: Johns Hopkins University Press, 1975) chap 7.
27. Leccese, "News" p. 9; Davis 'Fortress' p. 357

Bibliography

Bender, Thomas. *Toward An Urban Vision* (Baltimore, Johns Hopkins University. Press 1975).

Davis, Mike. "Fortress Los Angeles" in Philip Kasinitz, ed., *Metropolis* (NY: NYU Press, 1995).

Fabos, J. Et. Al. *F.L. Olmsted, Sr. Founder of Landscape Architecture* (Amherst: University of Massachusetts Press, 1968).

Fein, Albert *Frederick Law Olmsted and the American Environmental Tradition* (NY: Braziller, 1972).

Fisher, Irving D. *Frederick Law Olmsted and the City Planning Movement in the U.S.* (Ann Arbor: UMI Research, 1986).

Greene, Bradford M. *Staten Island Advance*, November 24, 1968.

Greene, Bradford M. "The Staten Island Improvement Commission of 1870" (part two) *Proc. Of Staten Island Institute of Arts and Sciences.* March 30, 1968.

Hall, Lee. *Olmsted's America* (Boston: Bulfinch Press 1995).

Leccesse, Michael. "News" *Landscape Architecture* (Jan. 95) p. 19.

Roper, Laura *FLO* (Baltimore: Johns Hopkins University Press, 1973).

Scheper, George L. "The Reformist Vision of F. L. Olmsted and the Poetics of Park Design," *New England Quarterly* (Mar.-Dec. 1989).

Starr, Roger. "The Motive Behind Olmsted's Park." *The Public Interest* (Winter 88).

Stevenson, Elizabeth. *Park Maker* (NY: MacMillan, 1977).

White, Dana *Frederick L. Olmsted-The Placemaker* in Daniel Schaffer, ed., *Two Centuries of American Planning* (Baltimore: John Hopkins University Press, 1988).

Edwin Arlington Robinson (1869-1935): Staten Island Reflections

Diana Gosselin Nakeeb

> There is an island
> Where men remember me; and from an island,
> Surprising freight of dreams and deeds may come.
> —E.A. Robinson, *Toussaint L'Ouverture*, 1932

The year 1913 of which the American poet Edwin Arlington Robinson spent the first three months on Staten Island, was in every sense a turning point in his life. He was 43 years old. He had written poetry all his life, and never made a dime from it. He had also done virtually nothing except write poetry. How did he manage that, before grants were invented? To quote from one of Robinson's poems about an imaginary character, "the man Flammonde:"

> And what he needed for his fee
> to live, he borrowed graciously.[1]

He was born into a well-to-do family in Maine in 1869, attended Harvard, but dropped out in his third year when the family went bankrupt. Both his parents soon died, followed by an older brother (who left behind a widow and three children), and EAR stayed in Maine for several years, trying to keep things together. He published his first, great book of poetry—*Children of the Night*—in 1898. It passed completely unnoticed. And so he came down to New York City, looking for employment.

He became more of a New Yorker than a New Englander, and in fact died here in 1935. From November 1903 until August 1904, he took a job on the NYC subway system, which was then in the process of being built. He was a timekeeper for the construction crews, and spent 12 hours every day under ground—clocking the men as they arrived, staying all day to make sure they didn't leave, and clocking them again at the end of their 12-hour shift. When he finally emerged himself, there was no daylight left, so he would hit all the bars in midtown Manhattan.[2]

When his section of the subway was finished, he was laid off. He lived off his subway savings while trying to concentrate on poetry again. And when his money was just about gone—in March 1905—he received a letter from Theodore Roosevelt, the President of the United States. Virtually nobody read Robinson's poetry. The book publishers, literary magazines, and mainstream magazines rejected it over and over and over. But a young lad named Kermit just happened to get a copy of Robinson's first, self-published volume, *Children of the Night* (which includes the now-famous anthology piece, "Richard Cory"), and loved it. Kermit Roosevelt made his father read it, and Teddy loved it. On that basis alone—with no recommendations from professional critics—TR wanted to help this poet, if possible.[3]

Since EAR wanted to stay in New York City, TR gave him a sinecure at the Customs House in lower Manhattan—which was then in its original Tammany-Hall splendor. Although the job was a sinecure, Robinson had expected to have at least some meaningful work to do, and was demoralized to find that no one would let him do anything [Figure 1].

Every day at 1 p.m. Robinson showed up at the Customs House, left an open copy of the *New York Times* on his desk in Room 408, and then hit every bar in lower Manhattan. It was a great relief to him when the

Figure 1.

sinecure came to an end as the Roosevelt administration came to an end.

Once again he lived first on savings and then on handouts. He accepted the help and hospitality of various patrons, *if* they appreciated his poetry. He would not accept help for any other reason. And he in turn supported a motley crew of ne'er-do-wells who were less successful than he was at winning friends. To quote further from his poem, "Flammonde:"

> He never told us what he was,
> Or what mischance or other cause
> Had banished him from better days
> To play the prince of castaways.
> Meanwhile he played surpassing well
> A part, for most, unplayable:
> In fine, one pauses, half afraid
> To say for certain that he played.

Because Robinson was not a fraud—he wrote great poetry, and could not do anything else—people willingly sheltered him. But it bothered him. In principle, he felt that he had to pay everything back, and so for several years he neglected poetry and turned to playwriting.

In his playwrighting phase Robinson spent much of his time in Brooklyn, which at the turn of the century had many small theatres and was the equivalent of off-Broadway. None of his plays were accepted, and his alcohol dependency was getting worse. With great reluctance, he spent the summer of 1912 at the MacDowell colony, an artists' colony in New Hampshire. Despite his misgivings that colonies were for ants and termites, the experience did him good He resolved to switch from being an alcoholic to being a workaholic. But in 1912 it was still just a

Figure 2.

resolution.

One of Robinson's major benefactors, Clara Potter Davidge (forever surnamed "the daughter of Bishop Potter") had been putting him up in a guesthouse on the grounds of her house in Washington Square. Clara was a wealthy widow in her early 50s who patronized mostly painters. Her selections were based upon mystical intuition and personal acquaintance: she had to sense what the artist had in him or her. She founded the original Madison Avenue Art Gallery, which survives to this day, though now at another address. To quote from a letter to the *New York Times* which appeared at the time of her death, and was signed by half a dozen artists:

> It was in this gallery that the first meeting of the American Painters and Sculptors was held, that meeting where liberal artists of varying efforts but of one hope for live art gathered. [She] was in entire sympathy with this movement and helped it in every way. From this meeting grew the exhibition at the Sixty-Ninth Regiment Armory *in 1913—the first exhibition of modern art held in this country*—the effects of which were far-reaching.
> ... [Clara's] *vitality,* her *splendid optimism*, are gone but the work she did is bearing fruit today, and we who *among others* benefitted by her generosity and her affection cannot let her pass without a public recognition of *our deep respect.* [Italics added][4]

In 1912, Mrs. Davidge married one of the artists to whom she was a benefactress–Henry Taylor. She sold her house in Washington Square and bought the Latourette house on Staten Island, in the neighborhood known as Huguenot. However, even though EAR's guesthouse was now sold out from under him, this quintessentially impractical poet still landed on his feet. Mrs. Davidge Taylor and her husband Henry took EAR to Staten Island with them, when they moved there in December of 1912.[5]

The Latourette site [Figure 2] has had various structures since 1700.[6] However, the imposing house where EAR stayed and which today serves as the Latourette Golf Course clubhouse, was completed in 1836. Along with the mansion went a reputed resident ghost, and all of the land which is now the Latourette golf course. There were great views and all the privacy one could want. There was no active, regular news reporting on the area in those days. To go to Latourette was to drop out of sight, thus making it a perfect retreat for the wealthy and bohemian.

Robinson stayed with the Taylors from December of 1912 through March of 1913. Thanks to the Taylors—and he gave them full credit—he overcame his drinking habit. Their method was naive, but it worked: in the evenings, when a thirst came over him, the Taylors talked. And talked. And talked. By their distracting him, he was able to quit permanently.

During his stay in Huguenot, Robinson followed a pleasant routine of rising late, having a light brunch, thinking about writing, finally doing some writing, and then taking a walk. Most often, he walked downhill to the lighthouse: the very same "Staten Island Lighthouse" which stands and is still in use, and is a five-minute walk from Latourette. The lighthouse had just been completed in 1909, and was state-of-the-art for that time [Figure 3].

In 1913, it was easy to visit the lighthouse, which is now closed to the public. Robinson befriended the lighthouse-keeper, a man named Moore, who was a retired seaman. Robinson got in the habit of lending him books, so that Moore could while away the time. Moore, only 35, had

Figure 3.

retired prematurely, because he had had a foot chewed off by a piece of machinery. Even though, from ground level, all that can be seen is an ocean of trees, from the top of the lighthouse one can plainly see the ocean. Since Robinson went down to the lighthouse often, to climb to the top and visit with Moore, he was vividly aware of Staten Island as an island.

Perhaps Moore reminded Robinson of a friend back home, a Capt. Israel Jordan who was lost at sea, about whom EAR published a poem in 1910:

> Gone—faded out of the story, the sea-faring friend I remember?
> Gone for a decade, they say: never a word or a sign.
> Gone with his hard red face that only his laughter could wrinkle,
> Down where men go to be still, by the old way of the sea.
> Never again will he come, with rings in his ears like a pirate,
> Back to be living and seen, here with his roses and vines;
> Here where the tenants are shadows and echoes of years uneventful,
> Memory meets the event, told from afar by the sea.[7]

Not far down from the lighthouse, in easy walking or horse-clopping distance, is St. Andrew's Episcopal Church [Figure 4]. Besides being extremely mystical and intuitive, Mrs. Taylor was still the daughter of an Episcopalian bishop. She would at least occasionally have visited St. Andrew's Episcopal Church (1712; restored after the fire of 1868) in Richmondtown. And since the Taylors felt a mission to "save" Robinson, they may have brought him to St. Andrew's a couple of times over the course of the three months that he was their guest. And he could hardly have missed this landmark on his exploratory walks. So he would have

Figure 4.

encountered a little of the local Staten Island population, in addition to the bohemian and artistic types that the Taylors often had as guests.

A few years later, in 1917, Jacqueline Klauber (who named both her Manhattan art gallery and her Tibetan museum by her pseudonym, Jacques Marchais) also moved into the neighborhood, literally a few yards from the lighthouse on Lighthouse Avenue. Since the founder of Staten Island's Tibetan Museum was every bit as mystical as Mrs. Taylor, one is tempted to surmise that she was led here by the vibrations alone. Of course, the site is not far from Emerson Hill, where the vibrations of Henry David Thoreau and the New England Transcendentalists—who incidentally were Robinson's favorite American writers—still linger [Figure 5].

Henry David Thoreau wrote of Huguenot in 1847 (based on material drafted in 1839):

> The hills in the interior of [Staten] Island, though comparatively low, are penetrated in various directions by sloping valleys, . . . gradually narrowing and rising to the centre, and at the head of these the Huguenots, who were the first settlers, placed their houses quite within the land, in rural and sheltered places, in leafy recesses, . . . from which . . . they looked out through a widening vista, over miles of forest and stretching salt marsh . . . .
>
> When walking in the interior there, in the midst of rural scenery, where there was as little to remind me of the ocean as amid the New Hampshire hills, I have suddenly, through a gap, a cleft, or "clove road" as the Dutch settlers called it, caught sight of a ship under full sail, over a field of corn, twenty or thirty miles at sea.[8]

An important decision that Robinson reached while living at Latourette was to turn his back on attempts to write a hit play or best-selling novel. Conscious that poetry meant "starving in a hole"—literally—he rededicated himself to poetry. The letter announcing his intention to do this was written from Latourette.

He also left the Taylors shortly thereafter, and never returned either to them or to Staten Island. Under circumstances never openly discussed, he broke with the Taylors completely. He dedicated both individual poems and whole collections to his other friends, but never any to them. However, the awkward situation of a married couple and a long-staying guest, all rattling around in a big house on an isolated, almost untouched, natural site is treated in several of Robinson's long narrative poems, which end with the suicide of one or more of the parties. The most significant are *Roman Bartholow* (1923) and *Matthias At the Door* (1931).

After 1913, Mrs. Taylor—formerly a very prominent patron of the arts—no longer appeared in the pages of the *New York Times*, until a sudden, shocking notice on Nov. 8, 1921:

> *Bishop Potter's Daughter Drowns: Body of Mrs. Henry Fitch Taylor discovered in marsh near her Long Island home.*
>
> The body of Mrs. Clara Sydney Taylor, a daughter of the late Bishop Potter, was found on Sunday morning in a marsh beside a private road leading from the cottage where she was living in the home of her brother, Alonzo Potter, at Smithtown, Suffolk County, L. I. Mrs. Taylor and her husband, Henry Fitch Taylor, an artist, had been living in the cottage on her brother's estate.
>
> She had been suffering from a spinal trouble, which caused her to walk unsteadily, and it is supposed that, while walking from her cottage to her brother's house, she had fallen into the marsh. As soon as she was missed, a search was started and she was found by her husband.[9]

The *Times* reporter is very obviously fascinated by the murky circumstances of this death, and makes no reference at all to Mrs. Taylor's years—formerly reported by the *Times*—of patronizing the arts. How she was reduced from the grand estate of Latourette to a cottage on her brother's property is also a mystery. But one suspects that Robinson's quarrel was, after all, with the unsuccessful artist Henry Taylor and not with his former benefactress.

After his fruitful stay on Staten Island, Robinson's fortunes took a turn for the better. By 1916, he published a major collection of poetry entitled *The Man Against the Sky*. The British critics recognized him first—thanks to a poem about William Shakespeare: *Ben Jonson entertains a man from Stratford*, in which Ben Jonson comes to life as a man who constantly refers to England, very comfortably and therefore convincingly, as "our island."

After the British recognition, Robinson began to get acceptances and interviews in America. And once this happened, his success as a poet was simply extraordinary. He won *three* Pulitzer prizes, his books became best-sellers, his complete works were issued and reissued, he was given munificent publishing contracts, and he paid off *all* his debts and gave everyone back their money. Just as he had always intended.

The evolution of Robinson's success parallels the evolution of his attitude towards islands. There is a great difference between his islands before and after 1913. A 1910 poem entitled "An Island (Saint Helena, 1821)" represents the very first time that Robinson attempted to describe an island. The poem is utterly negative, and regards "island" as synonymous with barren wasteland. Although he came from the coast of New England, and was familiar with oceanscapes and rivers, Robinson before 1913 had no feeling for islands, and they are missing from all of his poetry, except for perfunctory, imaginary references to the Greek isles. So in 1910, he attempted to convey the sense of an island when describing Napoleon's stay on St. Helena. But he had no concrete experience to go on, and his first island is completely abstract. It is, however, a suitable island for Napoleon—whom Robinson envisioned as a bombastic bully. Throughout the poem, a

Figure 5.

frustrated and angry Napoleon speaks for himself:

> "... Yes,
> There are too many islands in this world,
> There are too many rats, and there is too much rain.
> So three things are made plain
> Between the sea and sky:
> Three separate parts of one thing, which is Pain...
> Bah, what a way to die!" (10)

This was written when Robinson still drank heavily, and is not very good. However, the first island reference to appear *after* 1913 will suggest the area around Latourette :

> No sound of any storm that shakes
> Old island walls with older seas
> Comes here where now September makes
> An island in a sea of trees. (11)

The poem is "Hillcrest" (*The Man Against the Sky*, 1916) and was dedicated not to the Taylors, who had sheltered Robinson in Latourette, but to Mrs. MacDowell, the composer's widow who had just started the MacDowell colony. The MacDowell colony was—and is—in the forests of New Hampshire, to which Thoreau also makes reference in describing Huguenot. One finds Robinson's appreciation for the MacDowell colony, which sheltered him thereafter, effusive. But although the Taylors are never mentioned again in his published letters, and Staten Island is not mentioned by name, a warm recollection of an island comes through time and again. Since Staten Island was the only one on which Robinson ever lived (except for Manhattan, which he never thought of as an island, but as *The Town Down the River*), it was the only island of which he had a concrete, physical sense.

Toussaint L'Ouverture, published in 1932, is the answer and companion piece to Robinson's poem about Napoleon on St. Helena. While Napoleon's island is all rats and vermin and negativity, the island of Napoleon's opponent, Toussaint L'Ouverture (leader of a rebellion against French rule on the island of Haiti), is the embodiment of life and shelter.

The poem is somewhat unusual, in that here is a finally-successful poet, from a patrician New England background, projecting himself into the last hours of an African rebel slave, Toussaint. When the poem appeared in 1932, it was resoundingly ignored by the critics, despite the fact that Robinson was at that moment one of the most famous poets in America. Its themes and prophecies make it more understandable today than it would have been in 1932.

The poem takes the form of a monologue, in which Toussaint is trying to make sense of the betrayal that Napoleon has played upon him. Toussaint's uprising had apparently succeeded, and Napoleon invited him to come to France to draw up the terms of a settlement. Toussaint trusted the offer, was taken to France, and was immediately thrown into a jail, where he starved to death.

Because Toussaint, from the first word, addresses the reader directly, Robinson creates the illusion that this is not so much a monologue as a dialogue in which the reader is a silent partner. Toussaint asks us:

> Am I alone—or is it you, my friend?
> I call you friend, but let it not be known
> That such a word was uttered in this place.
>
> ... I did not know that there was anything left
> Alive to see me, or to consider me,
> As more than a transplanted shovelful
> Of black earth with a seed of danger in it —
> A seed that's not there now, and never was.
> When was I dangerous to Napoleon?
> Does a perfidious victor fear the victim
> That he has trapped and harassed? No, he hates him.
>
> There lives in hate a seed more dangerous
> To man, I fear, than any in time's garden
> That has not risen to full stalk and flower
> in history yet.[12]

Considering that this poem was published in 1932, Robinson had to have had fascism and racism in mind as well as the long-ago fate of Toussaint. As Toussaint continues, you can hear the island lilt in his voice—although Robinson does not *play* on that, and gives Toussaint a very classical idiom:

> I am glad now for being
> So like a child as to believe in him
> As long as there was hope. And what was hope?
> Hope was a pebble I brought here to play with,
> And might as well have dropped into the ocean
> Before there was a bitter league of it
> Between me and my island. It was well
> Not to do that. Not that it matters now.[13]

There are three elements of Toussaint with which Robinson was able to emphathize. The first was, literally, being trapped in a cold hole for a year—while he worked on the subway. The second, was knowing how it felt to have one's work and even one's existence ignored, and the struggle required to keep on existing in spite of that. And the third element is great nostalgia for an island, which Robinson easily enters into, although he had only one island to look back on. Toussaint continues:

> My friend, I do not hear you any longer.
> Are you still there? (Or)... have they invented
> A last new misery fit for the last days
> Of an old sick black man who says tonight
> He does not think that he shall have to live
> Much longer now? If there were left in me
> A way to laugh, I might as well be laughing
> To think of that. Say to Napoleon
> That he has made an end of me so slowly,
> And (so) thoroughly, that only God Almighty
> Shall say what is to say. And if God made him,
> And made him as he is, and has to be,
> Say who shall answer for a world where men
> Are mostly blind, and they who are the blindest
> Climb to cold heights that others cannot reach,
> And there, with all there is for them to see,
> See nothing but themselves. I am not one
> To tell you about that, for I am only
> A man destroyed, a sick man, soon to die;
> A man betrayed, who sees his end a ruin,
> Yet cannot see that he has lived in vain.(14)

This is a major poem—possibly Robinson's best, although it is almost unrecognized. In the conclusion, Toussaint's nostalgia for his *island* is absolutely fundamental to the poem's effect:

> Is this night?
> Or is it morning?. . . No, it is not night—
> For now I see. You were a dream, my friend!
> Glory to God, who made a dream of you,
> And of a place that I believed a prison.
> There were no prisons—no Napoleons.
> I must have been asleep for a long time.
> Now I remember. I was on a ship—
> A ship they said was carrying me to France.
> Why should I go to France? I must have slept,
> And sailed away asleep, and sailed on sleeping.
> I am not quite awake; yet I can see
> White waves, and I can feel a warm wind coming—
> And I can see the sun! . . . . This is not France—
> This is a ship; and France was never a ship.
> France was a place where they were starving me
> To death, because a black man had a brain.
> I feel the sun! Now we are going faster—
> Now I see land—I see land and a mountain!
> I see white foam along a sunny shore—
> And there's a town. Now there are people in it,
> Shouting and singing, waving wild arms at me,
> And crowding down together to the water!
> You know me—and you knew that I was coming!
> O you lost faces! My lost friends! My island!
> You knew that I was coming . . .
> You are gone.
> Where are you gone? Is this the night again?
> I cannot see you now. But you are there—
> You are still there. And I know who is here. [15]

Robinson was a quintessentially American writer, utterly dedicated to producing poetry that would not be provincial, yet would still be unmistakably American, with a "feel" and a "sound" that only an American background could provide. One may say that Staten Island—particularly the Huguenot region—played a modest, but distinct and essential role in helping Edwin Arlington Robinson to define and extend his sense of the American landscape. His Island sojourn also played a defining role in his personal biography, through his relationship with the Taylors, and the decisions about his life that he reached at that time. There is an interesting parallel between Robinson's Staten Island experience and that of another, very consciously American writer, Henry David Thoreau. Robinson was here for three months, and Thoreau for six. But though the time was short, both drank *in* their island experience intensely and at leisure; both were staying with very mystical or transcendental companions at the time; and the experience appears to have had great staying-power.

Notes

1. Robinson, Edwin Arlington. *Collected Poems* (New York: Macmillan, 1937), 3.
2. Hagedorn, Hermann. *Edwin Arlington Robinson: A Biography* (New York: Macmillan, 1938), 201-208.
3. Hagedorn, *op. cit.*, 212-218.
4. *New York Times*, Nov. 10, 1921. Signed by: George Bellows, D. Putnam Brimley, Walt Kulm, Ernest Lawson, Elmer Livingston MacRae, Jerome Myers, Allen Tucker.
5. Hagedorn, 280-283.
6. Steinmeyer, Henry G. *Staten Island: 1524-1898* (New York: The Staten Island Historical Society, 1950; revised, 1987), 29.
7. Robinson, *op. cit.*, 335.
8. Thoreau, Henry David. *A Week on the Concord and Merrimack Rivers* (Cambridge: Riverside Press, 1961), 190-191.
9. *New York Times*, Nov. 8, 1921.
10. Robinson, 324-325.
11. Robinson, 15.
12. Robinson, 1179-1180.
13. Robinson, 1180.
14. Robinson, 1181.
15. Robinson, 1186-1187.

Father John Christoper Drumgoole, Founder of Mt. Loretto: Understanding the Man

John J. Brennan

Father John C. Drumgoole (1816–1888), the nineteenth century Roman Catholic priest who founded Mount Loretto at Pleasant Plains on Staten Island, has been commemorated in many ways. Here on Staten Island, a street and a public school have been named after him. In Manhattan, there is a plaque in his memory at St. Peter's Church, and a square has been named for him near the foot of the Brooklyn Bridge. In Washington, D.C., there is another memorial at the Shrine of the Immaculate Conception. At Abbeylara in County Longford, Ireland, the land of his birth, St. Bernard's Church has been dedicated in his name.

A late vocation, Father Drumgoole was ordained a priest at the age of fifty-three on May 22, 1869. In late 1870, he was given full control as resident chaplain of the troubled St. Vincent de Paul Home at 53 Warren St. in Manhattan. He was so successful that in a short period of time it became necessary to expand the Home.[1] In 1874, he established St. Joseph's Union, which eventually became a worldwide organization, to finance the construction and maintenance of the Mission of the Immaculate Virgin on Lafayette St. in lower Manhattan. Considered a sky scraper at the time, it was occupied in December, 1881.[2] In June 1882, he arranged for purchase of the Bennett farm in Pleasant Plains, Staten Island, and it became the nucleus of Mount Loretto, which opened on November 29, 1883.[3] By 1886, Mt. Loretto was coed, and by 1887 its population outnumbered that at Lafayette St.[4] On Sept. 8, 1887, construction was begun on the Church of Sts. Joachim and Anne at Mt. Loretto.[5]

Yet, despite his accomplishments, Father Drumgoole remains shrouded in obscurity. An unusually humble man, he left no writings of a truly personal nature. The best source available is a diary written by a businessman named James Doherty, a longtime associate and trustee of the Mission. But even this contains no explanation of Father Drumgoole's actions, his spirituality or any inner conflicts.

Through the years, attempts have been made to recount the life of Father Drumgoole, most notably by Katherine Burton in her 1954 biography, *Children's Shepherd, The Story of John Christopher Drumgoole.* Devotional in its approach, it is true to available sources. However, it lacks an analysis of the person and a formal evaluation of the influences which shaped his ministry. Thus the questions remain. What were the most important influences in Father Drumgoole's emergence as a leading figure in child care in late nineteenth century New York City? How can one begin to describe his personal impact, given the nature of available sources?

Father Drumgoole arrived in New York City at the age of eight. Catholics then constituted about twenty percent of the city's population, and most of them were Irish.[6] As such, they were viewed as intruders in a Protestant land, and, lacking appropriate training, most of them were consigned to the non-skilled jobs of the day. They were at the lowest end of the social spectrum.

Irish Catholics, deprived as a group of opportunity and privilege in their homeland, knew well the arts of survival in a hostile environment. As a result of Cromwell's seventeenth century conquest, they had lost ownership of most of Ireland. In desperation, they had supported the Stuart candidacy of James II, only to be defeated at the Battle of the Boyne on July 14, 1689. In punishment and to deter future disturbances, a series of draconian measures known as the Penal Codes were passed through the Protestant-controlled Irish Parliament during the late seventeenth and early eighteenth centuries. These deprived Catholics of any opportunity whatsoever in their homeland, whether political, economic or social. Thus, although they composed the majority of the population, they became an oppressed minority, confined to the peasantry, separated from their nobility by religion and political allegiance, suffering the lowest standard of living in western Europe.[7]

During the late eighteenth century, a series of Relief Acts were passed through the Irish Parliament.[8] Together with the British Parliament's Catholic Emancipation Act of 1829, they relieved Catholics of the most pressing disabilities of the Penal Codes. However, many Penal Codes remained on the books, restricting public displays of religion, marriage rituals, church buildings, legal rights of religious orders, charitable activities and eligibility of Catholics for certain public offices.

Thus the benefits had been limited. Nevertheless, in the events which preceded Catholic Emancipation in 1829, a leader had emerged who became for the Catholic peasantry a legitimate model and folk hero. Daniel O'Connell, the Catholic Emancipator, formed the Catholic Association in 1823 to rally support for using legal means to remove disabilities on Irish Catholics. The cost of membership was one penny per month and funds raised were used to cover related expenses. Hundreds of thousands became involved, constituting a mass political movement,[9] giving Irish Catholics occasion to believe that it was possible for them to work effectively within the political system. In their optimism they would increasingly adopt use of the English language during the nineteenth century.

The Irish of the diaspora, including those in New York City, shared the euphoria generated by Daniel O'Connell, and young John C. Drumgoole spent his formative years in this environment. It is no accident that his St. Joseph's Union bears striking resemblance to Daniel O'Connell's earlier Catholic Association. In both cases, broad membership was obtained through the payment of a nominal fee, and the proceeds were used in the pursuit of each organization's goals. It is also worth noting that Father Drumgoole was willing to deal with public officials, even when he encountered anti-Catholic bias, and in doing so he was reflecting the spirit of Daniel O'Connell.

Father Drumgoole was also deeply influenced by the spirit of St. Vincent de Paul, the seventeenth century French priest who labored so successfully on behalf of the poor. St. Vincent ministered to those in need in a direct, personal way. Unlike most who had ministered to the poor before him, he sought ways to prevent poverty and social abuse and to enable the oppressed to help themselves. In these efforts, he enlisted the support of all people of good will, including the wealthy and privileged.[10]

Wherever St. Vincent de Paul, founder of the Congregation of the Mission, popularly known as the Vincentians, conducted missions of preaching and prayer, he founded Confraternities of Charity to provide opportunities for works of mercy. In 1833, Frederick Ozanam, a professor at the Sorbonne, revitalized the Confraternities, and the modern Society of St. Vincent de Paul was formed. By John Drumgoole's day it was the main instrument in Catholic New York City for raising funds and organizing large-scale efforts on behalf of those in need.[11]

Father Drumgoole studied under the instruction of the Vincentian fathers at Our Lady of the Angels Seminary in Niagara, New York; but he certainly had been familiar with the Society of St. Vincent de Paul's efforts even before he entered the seminary. In 1871, the Society appointed him to manage the St. Vincent de Paul Home on Warren St., and it was his primary source of funding until after he founded St. Joseph's Union in 1874. Indeed, his long-time collaborator, James Doherty, was a Vincentian.[12] Thus, Father Drumgoole's practical approach to problem solving and his ability to formulate large-scale plans resulted, at least in part, from his Vincentian education and the everyday influence of Vincentian clergy and laity.

Father Drumgoole's efforts on behalf of homeless children were preceded by those of the Protestant Children's Aid Society founded in New York City in 1853. Under the leadership of Rev. Charles Loring Brace, homeless youth were gathered into lodging houses, industrial schools, night schools, reading rooms and summer camps. The Society's programs were based upon late nineteenth century principles of self help, the gospel of work and the efficacy of education. At their lodgings, boys could obtain a bed, bath and supper for a nominal fee. They were taught to save their earnings and to read and write. Trade schools prepared them for employment; placement services aided in securing positions.[13]

Rev. Brace did not hold the youngsters accountable for their plight, believing that a wholesome environment would encourage the development of "temperance and virtue." He was also convinced of the importance of religious training, a fact much appreciated by Father Drumgoole who, on the other hand, vigorously opposed the Children's Aid Society's policy of relocating street children to foster homes in the South and West without regard to religious affiliation. It is estimated that, between 1853 and 1893, 91,536 youngsters were placed out of the city in this fashion, a practice which undoubtedly motivated the St. Vincent de Paul Society in New York City to open a Catholic home for boys in 1869. In all, however, Father Drumgoole found much in the accomplishments of the Children's Aid Society that was worthy of admiration, and he readily used their programs as models for his own.[14] In the process, he put his inimitable stamp on them, and in the final analysis his programs reflected his own distinctive personality.

Given the paucity of personal sources, efforts to understand Father Drumgoole must rely on indirect evidence. What follows, therefore, is an attempt, using contemporary references, to view the man from several distinct perspectives.

In view of his priesthood, it seems appropriate to begin with Father Drumgoole's spirituality. Accounts indicate that his primary acts of worship were daily celebration of the Mass and communal prayer with the children. When his busy schedule permitted—as during ferry trips to Staten Island—he recited the Rosary. Much of his private time during periods of stress was devoted to conversational-style prayer with St. Joseph, whose intercession he consistently sought on behalf of the children. He was aided in this practice by a statue of St. Joseph which he kept in his room and which is presently located in the Memorabilia room at Mt. Loretto. But while he prayed to St. Joseph for intercession, he recognized the position of the Blessed Mother as the foremost of all saints in naming his famous institution in her honor—The Mission of the Immaculate Virgin. Thus Father Drumgoole comes across as orthodox in doctrine, deeply committed to his faith, and, in keeping with the spirit of St. Vincent de Paul, engaged in a spirituality which took expression in good works rather than contemplation.[15]

Father Drumgoole was not one to be concerned with personal appearance or comfort. There are several references to his tattered clothing, and Burton's biography refers to him as "the shabby priest" in her account of his meeting with Cardinal McCloskey in 1875. As early as his seminary days, nuns would sew his buttons and attempt to repair his cloak and jacket when he visited them. From his first assignment on Warren St., he insisted on living with his charges, occupying a small, simple room with only a bed, composed of slats and a mattress of straw, and a desk and chair. He ate simply, sharing the diet of the children.[16]

Father Drumgoole's most distinctive characteristic was his total dedication to homeless children. He had realized this as a special calling even before entering the seminary in 1865, and he spoke about it during his seminary days. Two events in his life offer insight to the extent of his commitment. In August of 1874, he had become so inundated with responsibilities that for a time he lost track of his mother and learned of her final illness only after she had already been given the last rites. Two years later, on Christmas Day, 1876, he admitted to being tired "for the first time in his life." A doctor who attended him remarked that he had no apparent illness, but seemed "all worn out."[17]

Father Drumgoole's goals for his youthful charges were made clear through his public statements as well as his actions. In an interview with an official of the State Board of Charities, he spoke about his efforts to cultivate "self reliance and industry" in his boys so that they might become "honest and self-respecting" members of society.[18] He viewed homeless children as victims of society rather than culprits, blaming their condition on "neglect."[19] He sought to instill in them the personal pride which they needed for survival. In the matter of religious goals, he spoke often of how being faithful to God promoted faithfulness to one's country.[20]

The extraordinary emphasis which Father Drumgoole placed on patriotism was undoubtedly due to the sense of crisis which had emerged among many native Protestant-Americans following the influx of large numbers of non-Protestant immigrants from the 1840s onward. His youthful charges had to be prepared to demonstrate their loyalty if they were to be active participants in society. But, given the way he cherished his own citizenship, one has to suspect that personal affection for his adopted country was also involved. Special holiday events, such as the centennial celebration on July 4, 1876, were observed with profuse decorations and recitations of historic speeches and documents, such as the Declaration of Independence. On Thanksgiving in 1880, Father Drumgoole delivered one of his many patriotic addresses to his boys, saying in part, "When you grow old enough to vote, you must remember . . . that you are called on to defend by your votes . . . liberty . . . and thus uphold the honor and glory of your country." In 1884, another address included the exhortation that they should be prepared to fight for their country in war and vote for it in peace and the warning that "the man who barters his vote is a traitor . . . as a spy in war."[21]

Adversity was not a stranger. Described as a quiet man who rarely reacted to personal affronts but always defended children when they were mistreated or maligned,[22] he undoubtedly was provoked many times. Despite his early success at Warren St., he was subjected to constant criticism about his unorthodox managerial practices from his Vincentian benefactors.[23] On November 30, 1875, when police dispersed a gigantic fundraising meeting on the grounds that it involved gambling and was therefore illegal, he cooperated but noted that they could have notified him earlier.[24] In 1877, only one-third of the monies due from New York City were received, but there was no record of public reaction by him. It can be assumed that he worked quietly on this matter until by 1885 the Mission became the second highest private institution in receipt of public funds. Distressed over the bidding process for construction of the Lafayette St. building in 1879, he asked James Doherty to accompany him to Staten Island, saying "I've heard it's a pleasant place and I can get away from bids and bidders and friends of bidders for a few hours there." He held his ground and got the kind of building he wanted, "despite architects and contractors." He faced opposition from local inhabitants in Pleasant Plains, Staten Island, who disliked Catholic institutions to begin with, and feared the impact that a large influx of youngsters would have on the area as well. He was also confronted with fears that use of the beach area by the children might damage oyster beds off the coast.[25]

The most serious problems came toward the end of his life. A City Commissioner, Mrs. Josephine Lowell, was openly critical of him in 1886, citing the poor quality and small size of his managerial staffs and his lack of "manual and training programs," adding that "the present object seems to be to collect the greatest number possible and maintain them at the expense of private charity and public money and educate them to be good Catholics." Her remark that "I am sorry to say he considers me as something worse than a heathen . . ." reflects the tone of the forceful letter which he sent to her on this matter.[26]

Criticisms from fellow Catholics in Baltimore in 1887, on the other hand, provoked an open response in *The Homeless Child* issue of 1888-89, a publication addressed to benefactors of the Mission. Denying that he had ever used donations for his personal needs, Father Drumgoole insisted that receipts from St. Joseph's Union funds had been allocated solely for the children, the Mission itself and for foreign missionaries. Lest his readers still have doubts, he added that Mission property had already become an incorporated institution under the Archdiocese of New York and that all of his possessions would go to the Mission at his death. Finally, he wrote that most costs were being covered by St. Joseph's Union funds and that there were no outstanding debts.[27]

Father Drumgoole's humility and the simplicity of his lifestyle seem to run counter to his sophistication in dealing with members of the hierarchy. Early in his priestly career, he had his way with Archbishop

McCloskey, who permitted him to live with the children at Warren St. His meeting with the then Cardinal McCloskey in 1875 to gain permission for a larger building went quite smoothly. When he sought the aid of the Franciscan nuns of Buffalo to assist him at the Mission, he appealed with success for intervention by Bishop Ryan of Buffalo.[28] Still another meeting with Cardinal McCloskey was probably prompted by criticism that there was a lag in trade school or vocational programs. Again, Father Drumgoole handled himself well, citing his farming school at Mt. Loretto, his commercial classes at Lafayette St. and the need to give priority to construction of a church at Mt. Loretto.[29] His interest in the spiritual welfare of a Staten Islander named de Comeaus resulted from confidential inquiries about that gentleman from Cardinal McCloskey's successor, Archbishop Corrigan. He exchanged correspondence with Cardinal Parocchi, the Vicar of Rome, concerning plans for the new church which was to be modeled on St. Andrea della Valle in Rome, and even Pope Leo XIII offered advice about a painting which was to be located in the church.[30]

In his correspondence with Cardinal Parocchi, Father Drumgoole was quite eloquent when it came to describing the beauty of Mount Loretto. He was also very much at ease with important personages such as his unexpected visitor, Lord Rosebery, a British political leader and statesman of the day.[31] He was twice invited to address meetings of the Social Service Association at Saratoga Springs about issues related to child care. In 1883, he assured Archbishop Corrigan with surprising self-confidence that after the architects had studied specs of the best institutions in the country, it was he who personally selected the buildings for Mt. Loretto.[32]

Father Drumgoole's ideals, commitment, inner strength and skills—all were enhanced in their effectiveness by the fact that the children knew he truly cared for them. During his Warren Street days, newspaper reporters were struck by the affectionate greetings he bestowed on his "tough-looking boys." He could be visibly troubled when youngsters had to face separation from their siblings. For him, youthful street victims were always "my boys." Even while enjoying occasional outings, they were on his mind. Returning from his first trip to Staten Island in 1879, he said, "Someday we'll have a trip and bring them along." In the summer of 1885, when rain cancelled a steamboat outing, he lifted their spirits by leading them as in a parade, using his walking stick as a baton, to the tune of "Pop Goes the Weasel." In his last years, when he would arrive at Mt. Loretto from Lafayette St., the children would rush to greet him, clutching him and attempting to mount his shoulders. He never turned them away; he knew everyone and had something to say to each.[33]

The volunteers who supported him were sometimes frustrated. James Doherty complained that he employed some "queer characters."[34] Trustees of the Mission sometimes complained quietly among themselves about his unorthodox methods. To their consternation, the first edition of *The Homeless Child* was late because he insisted on writing all of it himself. When he first set out to visit the Bennett farm, which was for sale on the south shore of Staten Island, he never got there, visiting two communities of nuns on the north shore instead, much to the discomfort of James Doherty who accompanied him. A few weeks later, when he returned and found no one at the Bennett farm, he left a note "scribbled" on scrap paper and departed. But the sale followed, nevertheless.[35]

Father Drumgoole was well aware of the importance of volunteers. Even when police ended his fundraiser in 1875, he made the time to socialize with volunteers, despite his disappointment. The Doherty diary contains multiple references to the special efforts he made to express his appreciation to them.[36] In the final analysis, his style, though sometimes unorthodox, was successful, and needy children were helped on a scale that few if any had anticipated. Volunteers could take pride in being part of it all.

His simple pleasures came primarily from his achievements on behalf of the children. Still, although described as "tone deaf," he enjoyed music, choirs, bands and Irish tunes.[37] Asked if Irish music should be played on the occasion of Cardinal McCloskey's first visit to Lafayette St., he responded, ". . . all Irish music is sacred music."[38] Finally, he enjoyed and was comforted by the quiet and efficient support of the Franciscan nuns who had come from Buffalo to share his mission and follow his leadership.

Thus, there were several important influences on Father Drumgoole's emergence as a leading figure in the field of child care in late nineteenth century New York City. An immigrant who prized his American citizenship, he was nonetheless molded by his Irish Catholic background and especially by the spirit of Daniel O'Connell. As a result of his seminary education and his many contacts with members of the St. Vincent de Paul Society, he was also shaped by the methodology of St.

Vincent de Paul. Finally, contemporary Protestant social programs provided models for his own. However, it was Father Drumgoole himself who took the initiative and dedicated himself to the care of homeless youth in his own unique way.

Although he remains very much a private figure, several things are clear. It is impossible to separate him from his priesthood, so devoted was he to his religious calling. Rather than be concerned with his own comfort, he was totally dedicated to the children under his care. He preferred constructive reaction to adversity, in the process reflecting extraordinary courage and stamina. He led a simple, humble life, but he was not without the sophistication necessary for dealing with ecclesiastical superiors and public personalities and officials. His success with youngsters was enhanced by the unabashed affection he had for them. His ability to attract the service of able volunteers was mainly due to his successes, but also to the ways in which he displayed his appreciation toward them.

Today, although the role of the Mission of the Immaculate Virgin at Mt. Loretto has broadened to include a wide number of services to the Staten Island community, Father Drumgoole has not been forgotten. As Cardinal O'Connor said in 1994, during a Mass in celebration of the contributions of the Sisters of St. Francis, Father Drumgoole served a specific contemporary need. The need has changed, but his spirit lives on. In keeping with this reality, the Board of Trustees of the Mission has announced its intention to preserve its archives and artifacts of Father Drumgoole's life and to make them more accessible to the public. In this way, it is hoped that the man and his impact will be remembered so that others may be inspired to see the problems of the needy as their own.

Notes

1. George Jacoby, *Catholic Child Care in Nineteenth Century New York* (Washington, D.C.: Catholic Univ. of America Press, 1941), pp. 159-160.

2. Jacoby, pp.160, 164, 165. *The Homeless Child and Messenger of St. Joseph's Union*, 1870-1943, (New York: n.p.), 1876-77, p.3.

3. Marguerite Mahoney, "A History of the Mission of the Immaculate Virgin, Staten Island:1870-1945," Thesis: Fordham Univ., 1945, p.45. Jacoby, *op. cit.*, pp.165-166.

4. Katherine Burton, *Children's Shepherd*,(New York: P.J. Kennedy & Sons, 1954), pp.171, 176.
5. Mahoney, *op. cit.*, p.58. *The Homeless Child, op. cit.*,1888-89, p.4.
6. Burton, *op. cit.*, p.17.
7. Karl Bottigheimer, *Ireland and the Irish, A Short History* (N.Y.: Columbia Univ. Press, 1982), pp.129-144. R. Foster, ed., *The Oxford Illustrated History of Ireland* (Oxford Univ. Press, 1989), pp.163-166.
8. Bottigheimer, *op. cit.*, pp.150-157. Foster, *op. cit.*, p.184.
9. Donal McCartney, *The World of Daniel O'Connell* (Dublin & Cork: Mercier Press, 1980), p.30. R. Dudley Edwards, *Daniel O'Connell and His World* (London: Thames & Hudson, 1975), p.48. Foster, *op. cit.*, pp.184-186.
10. Daniel McColgan, *A Century of Charity* (Milwaukee: Bruce, 1951), I, pp. 1,11,17.
21. *Ibid.*,I, pp. 13-14, pp. 359-365.
12. *Ibid.* I, 357. Jacoby, *op. cit.*, p.164.
13. Miriam Langsam, *Children West: A History of the Placing-Out System of the New York Children's Aid Society* (Madison: State Historical Society of Wisconsin, 1964), pp. 9,11-12,13.
14. *Ibid.*, pp.15,25,47. McColgan, *op. cit.*, I, 363. Burton, *op. cit.*, pp.63,65. Jacoby, *op. cit.*, p.161. *The Homeless Child, op. cit.*, 1876-77, p.7.
15. Burton, *op. cit.*, pp.180,69,134,47. McColgan, *op. cit.*, I,17. *The Homeless Child, op. cit.*, 1876-77, p.7; 1889-90, p.4.
16. Burton, *op. cit.*, pp. 98,139,68,134.
17. *Ibid.*, pp.46,49,92,61. James E. Doherty, *Diary of James E. Doherty* (personal friend of Father Drumgoole), 1866-1897. (n.p,, n.d.), p.124A.
18. *The Homeless Child, op. cit.*, 1876-77, p.6.
19. *Ibid.*
20. *Ibid.*
21. Burton, *op. cit.*, pp. 109,138,169. *The Homeless Child, op. cit.*, 1889-90, p.13.
22. Burton, *op. cit.*, p.197.
23. *Diary, op. cit.*, pp. 113-118.
24. *The Homeless Child, op. cit.*, 1876-77, p.5.
25. Burton, *op. cit.*, pp. 105,107,120,178,128,135,162. *Diary, op. cit.*, p.145.

26. Burton, *op. cit.*, pp. 177-178. John C. Drumgoole, Letter to Mrs. Josephine Shaw Lowell. 6 January, 1886. Father Drumgoole Archives. Mt. Loretto, Staten Island.
27. *The Homeless Child, op. cit.*, 1887-88, p.8.
28. *The Homeless Child, op. cit.*, 1882-83, p.2.
    Diary, op. cit., p.142.
29. *The Homeless Child, op. cit.*, 1882-83, p.2.
30. Burton, *op. cit.*, pp. 101, 154, 169, 174, 181.
31. *Diary, op. cit.*, p.117.
32. Burton, *op. cit.*, pp. 181,113, 121,160.
33. *Ibid.*, pp. 81,95, 112, 129, 172-173, 179-180. *The Homeless Child, op. cit.*, 1883–84, p.2; 1889-90, p.2.
    Diary, op. cit., p. 136.
34. *Diary, op. cit.*, p.142.
35. *Diary, op. cit.*, pp. 131. Burton, *op. cit.*, p. 118.
36. *Diary, op. cit.*, p.147. Burton, *op. cit.*, pp. 153,107.
37. Burton, *op. cit.*, pp. 76,138.
38. *Diary, op. cit.*, p.142.

Bibliography

Bottigheimer, Karl. *Ireland and the Irish, A Short History.* New York: Columbia University Press, 1982.

Burton, Katherine. *Children's Shepherd.* New York: P.J. Kennedy & Sons, 1954.

Doherty, James E. *Diary of James E. Doherty (personal friend of Father Drumgoole), 1866-1897.* n.p., n.d.

Edwards, R. Dudley. *Daniel O'Connell and his World.* London: Thames & Hudson, 1975.

Foster, R. (ed.). *The Oxford Illustrated History of Ireland.* Oxford Univ. Press, 1989.

Jacoby, George. *Catholic Child Care in Nineteenth Century New York.* Washington, D.C.: Catholic Univ. of America Press, 1941.

Langsam, Miriam. *Children West: A History of the Placing-Out System of the*

New York Children's Aid Society. Madison: State Historical Society of Wisconsin, 1964.

McCartney, Donal. *The World of Daniel O'Connell.* Dublin & Cork: Mercier, 1980.

McColgan, Daniel. *A Century of Charity.* 2 vols. Milwaukee: Bruce, 1951.

O'Ferrall, Fergus. *Catholic Emancipation: Daniel O'Connell and the Birth of Irish Democracy, 1820-30.* Dublin: Gill & Macmillan, 1985.

Rosenwaike, Ira. *Population History of New York City.* Syracuse Univ. Press, 1972.

Magazine

The Homeless Child and Messenger of St. Joseph's Union, 1870-1943. New York: n.p.

Pamphlet

Father John C. Drumgoole. Pamphlet. n.p., 1989.

Thesis

Mahoney, Marguerite. "A History of the Mission of the Immaculate Virgin, Staten Island: 1870-1945" Thesis: Fordham Univ., 1945.

Letter

Drumgoole, John C. Letter to Mrs. Josephine Shaw Lowell. 6 January, 1886. Father Drumgoole Archives. Mt. Loretto, Staten Island.

Statue of Capt. Robert Randall at Sailors' Snug Harbor, Staten Island.

Sailors' Snug Harbor: A Microcosm of Turn-of-the-Century New York Politics

Geraldine A. Riley

At the turn of this century, Staten Island's small town atmosphere offered its inhabitants a welcome relief from the hectic existence of New York City. Local residents believed that problems associated with city life were left behind as ferries returned workers to their quiet island homes.

A short distance from those ferries was Sailors' Snug Harbor. Founded on an 1801 legacy provided by Captain Robert Richard Randall, the Harbor since 1831 had provided shelter for retired, indigent and infirm seamen. Islanders thought of Sailors' Snug Harbor as an isolated enclave having little if any impact on the surrounding community. Yet in the last decade of the nineteenth century the Harbor became the focus of a state-wide battle between Democrats and Republicans. The right of Harbor residents to vote was at the heart of this battle. What began as a movement to rid the Harbor of the illegal but commonplace activity of buying and selling votes, ended with the political and economic elite—read Republican Party—imposing the worst sort of exclusionary government on the residents of Sailors' Snug Harbor by denying them the right to vote.

This disenfranchisement was indicative of a larger political problem inherent in the development of late nineteenth century America: could democracy survive in a society grown more ethnically diverse and socially as well as economically stratified as a consequence of industrialization, urbanization, and mass immigration? The events at Snug Harbor were, in miniature, a reflection of this concern and a response to it.

The two major influences in the disenfranchisement of Snug Harbor residents were the political and economic elites. Late nineteenth century politics was dominated by a handful of economically advantaged individuals. In this regard, turn-of-the-century New York stands as a textbook example of elitism at work. As the prominent New York attorney Simon Sterne remarked, "We must stop organizing on the basis of arbitrary population and organize on the basis of interests."[1] Such a view translated into a narrowing perception of democracy with regard to who should be permitted to participate in government. Thus disenfranchisement was the result of a bias rooted in economics and realized through politics.

It is my belief that political and economic conditions of the period led to the disenfranchisement, an act which must be considered as extraordinary as the sale and purchase of ballots, in itself a fairly commonplace activity within the New York political arena. State legislation, whether approved or vetoed by various governors, indicates that the problem of selling ballots was widespread and engaged in by both Democratic and Republican political machines. Indeed, politicians so feared reprisals from the electorate that many refused to take the necessary steps to correct the problem.

With regard to Sailors' Snug Harbor, Ira Morris, a contemporary observer and author of *Morris' Memorial History Of Staten Island*, asserts:

> It is a notorious fact that to a certain member of each party was assigned for years the duty of purchasing the Harbor votes, and both General Committees considered it one of their most important necessities to make financial preparations for that purpose.[2]

The fierce competition for power and wealth between the Republican and Democratic machines was at the heart of the disenfranchisement as the two parties maneuvered for political advantage over one another. Disenfranchising an entire block of voters would secure a political advantage for the Republicans who at the stroke of a pen would remove from the electorate an entire block of staunchly Democratic voters.

The issues and circumstances of the day played a role in the fate of the Sailors' Snug Harbor residents. The effort to consolidate the New York bay area into what is today New York City appears to have had an important but indirect effect on the disenfranchisement. Initially it was thought consolidation would place at least partial control of New York City politics in the hands of the Republicans. On Staten Island this effort to increase Republican numbers ended in the obliteration of two historically connected democratic districts through investigations, indictments, and court cases spearheaded by independent Democrats and supported by Republicans. The main goal was to weaken the political supremacy of the Democratic machines in the New York City area.

Sailors' Snug Harbor under Gustavus Trask would find itself intimately caught up in these developments. Trask, a native of Massachusetts, was appointed Governor of the institution in 1884. Upon his appointment, Trask was informed by the Board of Trustees that for "25 years or more the Snug Harbor has been made an open market for the buying and selling of votes at local, state and national elections."[3] Apparently it was a problem which the Board of Trustees as well as previous governors could not or would not control. Testimony presented on May 6, 1890 to the Court of Oyer and Terminer in Richmond states:

> . . . previous to November 1884, money was openly paid for votes by politicians who carried leather bags with greenbacks and silver, which they distributed to the inmates outside and inside of the grounds of the Harbor. . . .[4]

As the situation at Sailors' Snug Harbor makes clear, the exchange of money for votes was a clear indication that a political machine was at work. M.R. Werner's *Tammany Hall* asserts that for the infamous New York political machine:

> The Monday before election day was known as . . . "Dough Day," for it was then that Tammany distributed the money that was to be spent in the election campaign of the next day.[5]

Besides the buying of votes, several other methods were used by machines to ensure victory. Stuffing ballot boxes and preventing the opposition from voting were two alternative methods. Both were employed by Tammany Hall as well as by the Muller machine on Staten Island.

While election frauds were a reality of nineteenth century New York State politics, it appears that the 1892 election was more corrupt than usual. David Hammack, in his *Power and Society—Greater New York at the Turn of the Century*, states: "By the early 1890s some wealthy Republicans, Democrats, and independents had resolved to pursue several political reform goals through nonpartisan, essentially pressure-group methods."[6] Staten Island was no exception, and on October 4, 1893, *The New York Times* announced a political movement had been started on Staten Island for the purpose of defeating the faction headed by Nicolas Muller.[7]

The Richmond County Democrats, an anti-machine branch of the Democratic Party, was founded and headed by Staten Island attorney Howard R. Bayne. Mr. Bayne, a native of Virginia, relocated to Staten Island in 1881.[8] On October 17, 1893 the Republicans and the Richmond County Democrats announced their intention to nominate a fusion ticket which would run in the November elections. Its goal was to defeat Boss Muller's machine.[9]

Nicolas Muller began his career as boss of the Democratic machine on Staten Island in the mid 1870s when he seized control of the party from Boss John G. Vaughn.[10] By all accounts Muller's "fighting qualities proved of great value to him. . . ."[11] *The New York Times* stated on October 26, 1893 that this boss was well-suited for Staten Island politics as he had "received his political education in the vicinity of Castle Garden under the auspices of the Tweed regime in New York."[12] And as Ira Morris observed, Muller came "from one of the shrewdest political schools in the world—that of Tammany Hall. . . ."[13] Schooled by Tammany, Muller was well-equipped to overcome any and all obstacles to his power on Staten Island.

Muller successfully ran his political machine from the mid 1870s into the first decade of the twentieth century. The last position he held was in 1908 when he served as Tax Commissioner for the Borough of Richmond.[14] The beginning of his downfall, however, can be traced to 1893 when *The New York Times* reported that Muller dismissed ". . . the County Engineer, and, in spite of the protests and petition of many citizens. . . ."[15]

In 1893, whether in response to Muller's refusal to acquiesce in the electorate's wishes or not, a portion of the Staten Island citizenry founded the Richmond County Democrats, an anti-machine party. Mr. Bayne, in an effort to prove the extent of fraud employed by the Muller machine,

> ... went to the polls ... the first registry day, with a witness, and had his name properly inscribed upon the registry roll, when the roll was examined ... his name was missing, as were also the names of other independents. ....[16]

Whether the Muller machine underestimated its opponent is unclear. What is certain, however, is that the incident resulted in a number of investigations, indictments, and court cases which ended in the disenfranchisement of the residents of Sailors' Snug Harbor and the sacrifice of many of the machine's men. As *The New York Times* reported On October 4, 1893,

> A political movement has been started on Staten Island for the purpose of defeating the faction headed by Nicolas Muller.... The new movement is the result of the dissatisfaction which is generally felt at the way Nicolas Muller has managed the offices over which he has control.[17]

This movement included disgruntled Democrats and Republicans who were determined to defeat Nicolas Muller and his machine. Howard Bayne's fusion ticket lost the November 1893 elections.[18] Fraud was so clearly obvious, however, that countywide electoral investigations were instigated. Given Sailors' Snug Harbor's reputation, the investigators focused their initial attention on that institution. The 1893 election, just like those in previous years, was fraught with fraud. The election results of the Eighth and Ninth Districts of Sailors' Snug Harbor demonstrated the extent of the abuse.

Mr. Bayne led this investigation, in cooperation with the Sailors' Snug Harbor Visiting Committee. The result of that investigation indicated, in particular, that the Ninth District, along with the Eighth District was comprised mostly of Sailors' Snug Harbor residents. In the Eighth District, it was seen that of the 191 votes cast, 11 were cast by residents who in fact did not vote at all; 3 were cast by residents who were absent from the Harbor at the time of the election; and 3 were cast by individuals who were unknown to Harbor officials—thereby giving the Harbor's Eighth District 17 invalid votes. The 17 invalid votes credited to the Eighth District accounted for approximately 10 percent of votes cast above and beyond the legal number of registered voters.

116 Community, Continuity and Change

In the Ninth District the abuses were much worse. Forty-two votes out of 247 were cast by residents who did not vote at all; 10 votes were cast by residents who were dead or absent from the Harbor at the time of the election; 21 votes were cast by residents unknown to Harbor officials; and 1 vote was credited to a Ninth District resident whose ballot was in fact destroyed. Thus the Ninth District had 74 invalid votes which accounted for 43 percent of illegal votes. Together the Eighth and Ninth districts had a total of 91 illegal votes, or 26 percent of all votes cast.[19]

The court cases involving Sailors' Snug Harbor with regard to this scandal began in February 1894—just three months after the November election. By October of 1895 the courts had ruled that the residents could no longer vote. Several factors determined this outcome. As a matter of law, Justices Cullen and Gaynor, the two State Supreme Court judges who heard these cases, ruled in response to an amendment added to the State Constitution during the State Convention of 1894. The amendment read:

> For the purpose of voting, no person shall be deemed to have gained or lost a residence by reason of his presence or absence while employed in the service of the United States, *nor while engaged in the navigation of the waters of this State or of the United States or of the high seas,* nor while a student of any seminary of learning, *while kept at any almshouse or other asylum or institution wholly or partly supported at public expense or by charity,* nor while confined in any public prison.[20]

According to *The New York Times*, "The two institutions that were specially aimed at in this proposition were the Sailors' Snug Harbor on Staten Island, and the Soldiers' Home at Bath."[21] As the residents of the Harbor spent years at sea, they had no legal residence prior to admission to the home; and because of the amendment, it was deemed not one man gained a legal residence by entering the Harbor. In essence, the residents were considered indigents; and therefore, ineligible to vote. The state legislature specifically passed this amendment so that the residents of Sailors' Snug Harbor legally could be denied the right to vote.

Several factors determined the passage of this particular act. The rulings of both Justices Cullen and Gaynor reflected not only adherence to a questionable state Constitutional amendment, but also the politics of the period. 1894 marked the year Republicans ". . . gained the upper hand in politics throughout the state."[22] A key player in shaping the course that events took was the Republican Levi Morton who defeated Democrat David Hill for the governorship, thereby placing a powerful opponent of Democratic policy at the head of the state government. The amendment's passage promoted the ascendancy of Thomas Platt as head of the Republican machine in New York State. The Republican dream to destroy the Democratic hold over New York City politics through consolidation expanded. All of the above entered into the passage of the amendment. Disenfranchisement for the Sailors' Snug Harbor residents followed shortly thereafter.

Since consolidation was largely a Republican goal, it is logical to assume that Platt and his Republican machine were working toward achieving its realization in 1894. For them consolidation was

> . . . designed in part to restore the Republican Party's reputation in Brooklyn; the borough system might also give scope for Republican ambitions in Queens, on Staten Island, and even in the Bronx, where Republicans hoped to elect officials in years when they failed to elect the mayor.[23]

"Behind Platt's decision to support the bill was his conviction that the enlarged city would be ruled by commissions that would be appointed by the governor and staffed by Republicans."[24] By restoring the Republicans' reputation within the boroughs, Platt hoped to secure a Republican gubernatorial seat generated by the enormous constituency that a Greater New York would create. Then, through Republican-run commissions, Platt and his party would control the entire state machinery.

Traditionally New York City and the outlying areas voted Democrat. Hopefully a greater New York would assure the Republicans at least partial control of the city in years when a Democratic mayor had been elected. On Staten Island, a Democratic stronghold, Republicans needed to break the Muller machine. This was to be accomplished by the Republicans in alliance with Howard Bayne's reform party. The goal was to discredit and expose Muller and his machine in the hope of gaining votes from disgruntled Democrats while maintaining their own party's electorate. In doing this, the Republicans hoped to ensure a victory in the next election. Platt's dream of consolidation, and at least partial control of the city machinery, would then be realized.

While party politics and Republican ambitions were significant background factors to disenfranchisement, there were additional ones.

David Hammack contends in *Power and Society—Greater New York at the Turn of the Century*, that "Some prominent members of New York's economic elite disliked the limits which they believed poor voters imposed on their power."[25] These patricians saw their power and influence slipping to an ever-increasing number of non-English speaking immigrants and an ever-increasing number of poor. As Simon Sterne archly remarked, "applying the doctrine of universal suffrage . . . puts the taxpayers at the mercy of the taxeaters."[26] In this instance, democracy was seen as a narrow, and self-serving enterprise. Essentially the disenfranchisement of Sailors' Snug Harbor residents demonstrates that social tensions and concerns did have political consequences.

Hammack continues:

> Schemes to restrict the franchise to property owners or at least to those literate in English, and to impose stiff requirements on eligibility for the civil service, were the two political reforms that found most universal support among Greater New York's economic elites.[27]

These two issues, however, reflect two overriding social problems of the day—one of an increasing influx of non-English speaking immigrants into the city population; and the other of what to do with the poor in a city of expanding yet unequally distributed, wealth. Both of these forces, immigrants and the poor, were historically connected with the Democratic machine. Therefore, in an effort to deflect the increasing influence of these two groups, the Republican elite saw the destruction of the machines and disenfranchisement of the poor as solutions to the dilemma. Sailors' Snug Harbor residents presented an easy target. In reality, the problems which the New York City area was experiencing were inherent in a system of vast economic inequality. In a city such as New York, which was changing and expanding faster than society itself could control or comprehend, simple solutions sometimes appeared to present the clearest answers. In hindsight, however, the problems associated with turn-of-the-century New York appear to have been more economic than political. Solutions were sought in the political arena; and in the end society chose to address the effects of the problems rather than the root causes. These solutions had a direct effect on society as a whole, and on the residents of Sailors' Snug Harbor in particular. Thus the actions of the political and economic elite can be seen to have had an immense social effect on late nineteenth century New York.

Albert Shaw, a businessman and a member of the committee which studied the feasibility of consolidation, connects all the political and economic aspects of the era into one succinct statement. He believed, ". . . the choice of [elected officials] of the . . . cities should be lodged with the taxpayers."[28] In essence, the opinions and rights of the economically disadvantaged, "taxeaters" as attorney Simon Sterne called them, should be silenced with regard to any and all political, financial, and social programs which city governments might choose to impose. According to Mr. Shaw, those who do not pay taxes, or in the case of the residents of Sailors' Snug Harbor those living at the expense of others, should not share in the electoral process.

By 1895, the court cases involving the ex-sailors' right to vote had reached the New York State Supreme Court in Brooklyn. Justice William J. Gaynor, hearing the case ruled that the inhabitants of Sailors' Snug Harbor ". . . were not qualified voters. . . ."[29] as their circumstances directly related to the 1894 Constitutional Amendment holding ". . . that the inmates of institutions supported wholly or partly by charity shall not gain or lose a residence by reason of their being inmates of such an institution..."[30] The case did not end in Judge Gaynor's courtroom.

Professor Charles A. Collins, retained by the Democratic State Committee, questioned in an appeal to the Court whether the amendment was retroactive. Judge Edgar M. Cullen ruled it was:

> I think the present provision of the constitution is general and applies to all inmates of the harbor, whether they had acquired voting residence at the town or district in which the harbor is situated prior to the adoption of the constitutional amendment or not.[31]

An 1895 article in the *Brooklyn Eagle* reported:

> The mischief which the constitution intended to remedy was the participation of an unconcerned body of men through the ballot box, in municipal affairs, in whose further conduct they have no interest and from the mismanagement of which, by the officers, their ballots might elect, they sustain no injury.[32]

This final indictment holds a storehouse of information regarding why the disenfranchisement of the sailors occurred. It is clear the ruling sought to punish the residents for past illegal acts. Yet the buying and selling of votes was not uncommon to the era. Why, then, were the residents of Sailors' Snug Harbor singled out? It is possible the courts wanted to have these residents serve as an example of what could happen to others. However, such an explanation is too simple. Since both the amendment directed at these men specifically and the move to consolidate the Bay area originated in the state legislature, it is more appropriate to seek the answers there. Besides the fact that these men were singled out simply because targeting them was easy, it is more likely the move to disenfranchise the residents was the quickest and easiest method by which to achieve a Republican representation in city politics. Disenfranchisement, then, served two purposes. First, Republicans were provided with a successful outcome, with little time, energy, and money spent; and, secondly, disenfranchisement placated the fears the economic elites had of being overpowered by the poorer elements of society.

In his *The Memorial History of Staten Island*, Ira Morris states that it was "One of the greatest scandals that ever cursed the politics of Staten Island . . ." and hence it became "the last campaign in which the inmates of the Sailors' Snug Harbor voted. . . ."[33] The residents of the Harbor were mere pawns in turn-of-the-century New York politics and victims of economic bias. Because those against them were more politically and economically powerful, the residents were denied their right to vote—the most basic right any citizen has in a democracy. As the economic and political elites exerted their unchecked power, society as a whole stood dangerously close to becoming an exclusive rather than an inclusive entity. Turn of the century New York came very close to becoming a government comprised only of the privileged and powerful.

Notes

1. David C. Hammack, *Power And Society-Greater New York at the Turn of the Century*, (New York: Russell Sage Foundation, 1982), p. 201.
2. Ira K. Morris, *Morris's Memorial History of Staten Island,* (Staten Island: privately printed, 1900), p. 257.
3. Barnett Shepard, *Sailors' Snug Harbor 1801-1976*, (New York: Publishing Center for Cultural Resources, 1979), p. 25.
4. Trustees of Sailors' Snug Harbor, Court of Oyer and Terminer Papers, May 6, 1890, (Sailors' Snug Harbor Collection, U.S. Maritime College, Bronx, New York).
5. M.R. Werner, *Tammany Hall*, (New York: Doubleday, Doran & Co., Inc., 1928), p. 293.
6. Hammack, op. cit. p. 140.
7. *The New York Times*, "Tired of the Muller Machine," 4 October 1893, p. 8.
8. Charles Leng and William T. Davis, *Staten Island and Its People*, p. 32.
9. *The New York Times*, "Combined Against the Ring," 17 October 1893, p. 3.
10. Morris, op. cit. p. 256.
11. Morris, ibid., p. 258.
12. *The New York Times*, "'Ring' Rule on Staten Island," 26 October 1893, p. 5.
13. Morris, op. cit. p. 258.
14. Leng, op. cit. p. 362.
15. *The New York Times*, "Tired of the Muller Machine," 4 October 1893, p. 8.
16. *The New York Times*, "Object to Being Watched," 25 October 1893, p. 2.
17. *The New York Times*, "Tired of the Muller Machine," 4 October 1893, p. 8.
18. Leng, op. cit. p.32.
19. Visiting Committee, Summary of Poll Lists for Eighth and Ninth Districts, Sailors' Snug Harbor Collection, U.S. Maritime College, Bronx, New York.
20. *The New York Times*, "Delegates Still Talking," 21 August 1894, p. 2.
21. *Ibid*, p. 2.
22. Hammack, op. cit. p. 214.

23. Hammack, op. cit. p. 225.
24. David M. Ellis, James A. Frost, Harold C. Syrett, and Harry J. Carment *A History of New York State*, Ithaca: Cornell University Press, 1967), p. 379.
25. Hammack, op. cit. p. 7.
26. Ibid, p. 9.
27. Ibid, p. 316.
28. Ibid, p. 201.
29. *The New York Times*, "Can Snug Harbor's Sailors Vote?," 30 October 1895, p. 7.
30. *The New York Times*, "Delegates Still Talking," 21 August 1894, p. 7.
31. *Brooklyn Eagle*, "Snug Harbor Tars Can't Vote," 30 October 1895, no page available.
32. *Ibid.*
33. Morris, op. cit. p. 257.

Bibliography

Books
Morris, Ira K, *Morris's Memorial History of Staten Island,* Staten Island: Privately Printed, 1900.

Secondary Sources
Ellis, David M, James A. Frost, Harold C. Syrett, and Harry J. Carmen, *A History of New York State*, Ithaca: Cornell University Press, 1967.

Ellis, Edward Robb, *The Epic of New York City, A Narrative History*. New York: Old Town Books, 1966.

Hammack, David C, *Power and Society—Greater New York at the Turn of the Century.* New York: Russell Sage Foundation, 1982.

Leng, Charles W. and William T. Davis, *Staten Island and its People—A History 1609-1929*. New York: Lewis Historical Publishing Co, Inc, 1930.

Shepherd, Barnett, *Sailors' Snug Harbor 1801-1976*. New York: Publishing Center for Cultural Resources, 1979.

Werner, M. R, *Tammany Hall*. New York: Doubleday, Doran & Co. Inc, 1928.

Collection
Sailors' Snug Harbor Collection. Bronx: U.S. Maritime College

Newspapers
Brooklyn Eagle   10/31/1895   "Snug Harbor Tars Can't Vote"

The New York Times
10/04/1893	"Tired of the Muller Machine"
10/17/1893	"Combined Against the Ring"
10/25/1893	"Object to Being Watched"
10/26/1893	"'Ring' Rule on Staten Island"
08/21/1894	"Delegates Still Talking"
10/21/1895	"Can Snug Harbor Sailors Vote?"

New Brighton: Some Notes on Diversity

Richard B. Dickenson

Although frequently depicted as a homogeneous community, Staten Island has long been ethnically diverse and racially mixed. Only recently, however, have we become fully conscious of the reality of this. Awareness of issues of multiculturalism and diversity have helped writers, scholars, even the general public to discover the invisible or hear the silent. The Staten Island past is not unlike the American past as a whole: once the angle of one's vision shifts or the range of one's hearing is recalibrated, different voices and different faces, there all along, suddenly stand out with a new clarity.

One outstanding example of this long standing ethnic and racial diversity is the north shore community of New Brighton. An integral part of the North Shore coastline, New Brighton was named in 1835 by William E. Davis, an English developer, to evoke the image of Brighton, the elegant Regency-style seaside resort on the English Channel, south of London. Though for many centuries little more than a fishing village, Brighton by the 1830s was, thanks to the patronage of George IV, in its heyday. Davis, wishing to attract buyers to his new real estate enterprise on Staten Island, sought to copy some of the celebrated characteristics of the original Brighton.

The New Brighton that developed during the course of the nineteenth century was more than a salubrious seaside resort for the affluent. Economic development and immigration would both alter the neighborhood. Even at the time Davis laid out his plans, the township of Castleton (with which the village of New Brighton would become coextensive in 1860) was racially mixed. The 1820 census recorded the presence of 110 slaves and 11 free persons of color. Ten years later—manumission having come to New York in 1827—the 1830 census noted that 134 free blacks lived in the area. Still "New Brighton," with most residents of Anglo-Saxon or Dutch background, did not possess the mix of ethnic groups we now take for granted.

The social and political upheavals that convulsed Western Europe in the 1830s and 1840s led to a rise in the number of immigrants crossing the Atlantic. Economic opportunity drew many to New York; a fair number of these began to settle in North Shore communities. The Richmond County census of 1850 notes the increasing ethnic mix of Staten Island, most notably Irish and German (Italian, also, after 1880). These immigrants provided a workforce for such New Brighton industries as J. B. King's Windsor Plaster Mills (established in 1876 and bought by U.S. Gypsum in 1924); or the nearby Muralo Company; and Crabtree and Wilkinson, manufacturers of colorfully printed silks, locating to Jersey Street in 1844 and employing almost two hundred workers within a decade.

We do not possess figures for the ethnic breakdown of employees in these concerns. Historical indications are that New Brighton factory employment—as was true elsewhere—was largely white, primarily Irish. Given the small percentage of black workers (1.8% in 1890, down from 5.5% in 1830), even domestic service was a largely Irish and Scandinavian occupation. This pattern does not hold when we examine hotels and restaurants. The most prevalent occupation for African-Americans in Castleton during the nineteenth century was waiter. The Pavillion Hotel had a large contingent of black employees, many of whom came from the South. They served the seaside tourist trade in the restaurants as well as provided other forms of hotel service.

Houses of worship can also be a measure of the identity of a community. Today, if we look at the New Brighton area, we can see a range of religious choices, from stately edifices representing mainline Protestant denominations to storefront churches along Jersey Street serving black and Hispanic congregations. Albanian Muslims are even constructing a mosque and community center in the neighborhood. All of this is of course very different from a hundred years ago when black Protestants living in the area had to be marginal members of white churches (for example, the Brighton Heights Reformed Church or Christ Church).

Memories

The recollections of septuagenarian John J. Murphy, who worked with his Irish immigrant father maintaining the homes of well-to-do islanders such as Edward Flash of the Cotton Exchange, "Gugy" Irving of the Henderson Estate Co, and J. C. Runkle of the Warren Chemical Company, illustrates the symbiotic relationship between Irish Catholics and affluent Protestants. Mr. Murphy could point to the power some Irish were able to acquire as politicians and building and transportation leaders. Yet at the same time they were "restricted"— "Catholics need not apply"—from jobs with Proctor and Gamble or other corporate employers well into the early years of the twentieth century.

The members of the Marotta family, now advanced in years, have seen in their lifetimes the rise of New Brighton Italians such as NY State Senator John Marchi and Surrogate Judge Charles J. D'Arrigo into the political and social life of the borough, mirroring to some extent the Irish achievement. Overcoming initial discriminatory obstacles, these two groups led the way in the inculcation of cultural and ethnic diversity in the life of the Borough of Staten Island. It may be but a matter of time for their example to become a model for other racial, ethnic and religious groups to achieve the same levels of inclusion.

Appendix

Continuity, Community and Change: New Perspectives on Staten Island History
October 20, 21, 22, 1995

Friday, October 20, 1995

Keynote Address
Panel A. Sailors' Snug Harbor: A World Within a Fence
Commentator: Barnett Shepard, Staten Island Historical Society
Moderator: David Ward, MFA, Yale University; Snug Harbor Cultural Center
Harvey J. Weber, St. John's University
"Sailors' Snug Harbor: A Case Study of 19th Century Homelessness"
Geraldine A. Riley, College of Staten Island
"Sailors' Snug Harbor: A Microcosm of Turn of the Century New York Politics"

Saturday, October 21, 1995

PANEL B. *Staten Island Neighborhoods: Creating a Sense of Place*
Commentator: Dr. Daniel Kramer, College of Staten Island
Moderator: Dr. Robert Cuervo, St. John's University
Dr. Irene Dabrowski, St. John's University
"Local Needs and Citizen Leadership: The Strategies of Community Organization and Neighborhood Maintenance on Staten Island"
Dr. Anthony Haynor, Seton Hall University
"Rosebank: An Ethnic History"

PANEL C. *Diversity and Inclusion:*
African American Communities on Staten Island
Commentator: Michael Rosenfeld, Pace University
Moderator: Dr. Louis Foleno, St. John's University,
    College of Staten Island
Dr. William Askins, The Literacy Assistance Center
"Race, Class and Community in 19th Century Staten Island"
Richard Dickenson, Staten Island Borough Historian
"New Brighton Perspectives on Diversity Through Maps and Memories, 1834-1994"
Dr. Patricia Gloster-Coates, Pace University
"History of the Black Church on Staten Island, 1890-1994"

PANEL D. *Staten Island: History and Imagery*
Commentator: Dr. Cynthia Ward, New York University
Moderator: Dr. Lucy Bowditch, College of St. Rose
Professor Michael Rosenfeld, Pace University
"Staten Island Historians and the Arcadian Myth"
Dr. Diana Gosselin Nakeeb, Pace University
"Reflections of Staten Island in the Work of Edward Arlington Robinson"
Charles L. Sachs, South Street Seaport Museum
"The Island Image: Reflections and Refractions from Home and Abroad

PANEL E. *History Creates Community*
Commentator: Michael Rosenfeld, Pace University
Moderator: Michael Marino, St. John's University

Randall C. Brown, Independent Scholar
"The Early History of Staten Island, 1609-1664"
Dr. Charles LaCerra, College of Staten Island
"Some Industries on Staten Island in the 19th Century"
Dr. John Brennan, St. John's University
"Community and Caring: Father John C. Drumgoole, Founder of Mount
    Loretto, The Man and His Impact"

PANEL F. *Transportation and the Shaping of Staten Island*
Commentator: Dr. Jerome Krase, Brooklyn College
Dr. Joseph Bongiorno, St. John's University
"A History of the Staten Island Railroad Since 1836"

Sunday, October 22, 1995
PANEL G. *Community and Change: Staten Island Architecture and Urban Development*
Commentator: Dr. Phil Sigler, College of Staten Island
Moderator: Dr. Paul Patane, Fordham University

Dr. Howard Weiner, College of Staten Island
"Nineteenth Century Urban Planning in the Work of Frederick Law Olmsted"
Albert Melniker, A.I.A
"Staten Island Architecture, Past, Present and Future"
Barnett Shepard, Staten Island Historical Society
"Daniel D. Tompkins: A Staten Island Developer, 1815-1825"

PANEL H. *Neighborhood Public Art Projects Round Table*
Moderator: Olivia Georgia

Notes on Contributors

John J. Brennan, Director of the Honors Program at the Staten Island Campus and Associate Professor of History, has served St. John's University as an academic dean and assistant vice president. He studied Theology at the Gregorian University in Rome, Italy and holds the PhD in History from Fordham University. He is a past officer of Community Planning Board #3 of Staten Island and past President of the Village Green Resident's Organization in Arden Heights. A member of Holy Child Parish in Eltingville, he is presently President of the Board of Trustees of the Mission of the Immaculate Virgin, Mount Loretto.

Richard Dickenson is an authority in urban affairs and city planning. A graduate of Springfield College and Michigan State University, he studied town and country planning at the London School of Economics. He has served as borough historian of Staten Island since 1991.

Patricia C. Gloster-Coates, the author of "A History of the Black Church on Staten Island," has explored research on Muslims, Christians, and traditional African religions in her writings as a graduate student, associate professor of history, and a former director of Christian Education for the Protestant Episcopal Church, U.S.A. at St. Louis, Missouri; Washington, D.C., and New York City. Growing up in Pittsburgh, Pennsylvania in a home in which her father belonged to the National Baptist Church and her mother belonged to the Protestant Episcopal Church, she developed an appreciation for respecting religious tolerance. She currently teaches African History, African-American History, South African History, and North African History at the Pace University campus in New York City.

Charles LaCerra is Professor Emeritus of the College of Staten Island, CUNY. At CSI he taught history courses, especially focusing on American immigration and Italian American History. Professor LaCerra earned his B.A. from St. John's University, his M.A. from Hunter College and his PhD from New York University. He has published numerous articles and several books. His most recent book is titled *Franklin Delano Roosevelt and Tammany Hall of New York*. Professor LaCerra co-chaired the committee that planned the weekend symposium at Snug Harbor on the history of Staten Island in 1995.

Diana Gosselin Nakeeb is a linguist and poet who has lived on Staten Island since 1974. She has been an adjunct faculty member in the Department of Modern Languages at Pace University since 1984, teaching Russian language and literature, and the cultural history of Eastern Europe. She received her doctoral degree from Columbia University in 1972 for her dissertation on Dostoevsky and Balzac (*The Earliest Dostoevsky*). She has also worked in publishing and as a translator. She is currently working on a series of articles on the origins of the Balts and the Slavs, of which the first installment, "Another Window on the Prehistory of Baltic and Slavic," is being published by the *Journal of Baltic Studies*.

Geraldine A. Riley was born, raised, and continues to live on Staten Island with her daughter, Cortney. A graduate of Port Richmond High School in 1988, Ms. Riley returned to school and received her Bachelor of Arts Degree in history in 1992 from the College of Staten Island. In 1995 she earned her Master's Degree in Liberal Studies from that institution. The college awarded both degrees with honors. Currently Ms. Riley continues to research independent projects in the history of Staten Island. She hopes one day to pursue a doctorate in American History with a focus on the nineteenth century.

Michael Rosenfeld teaches modern European and American history at Pace University where he is also Associate Director of the University's Honors Program. He has written widely on local history, pedagogical issues, cultural concerns, and British Studies, and has lectured on these interests in Europe and South America.

Charles L. Sachs (B.A., Columbia University; M.A., SUNY, Cooperstown Graduate Program), formerly Chief Curator at the Staten Island Historical Society, Historic Richmond Town, is the author of *Made on Staten Island: Agriculture, Industry, and Suburban Living in the City* and *The Blessed Isle: Hal B. Fullerton and His Image of Long Island, 1897-1927* as well as other works on Staten Island history and the material culture and historical photography of the New York metropolitan region. He served as an Associate Editor for *The Encyclopedia of New York City*. He is currently Senior Curator of the New York Transit Museum. From 1993 through 1996, he served as a Commisioner on the New York City Landmark Preservation Commission.

Howard R. Weiner is an Associate Professor of History at the College of Staten Island. He teaches urban history courses including the History of Staten Island. Professor Weiner has published studies of new towns and urban media. Professor Weiner was a Fullbright scholar at the University of Rome and is a specialist in Italian and Italian-American History. He was an associate editor of the *Encyclopedia of New York City* and is a member of the Columbia University "Seminar on the City." Professor Weiner received his BA and PhD from New York University and his MA from Columbia. He is currently working on a study of American retirement communities.

Index

Abyssinian Baptist Church 19
Addams, Jane 78
African Methodist Episcopal Church 18
African Methodist Episcopal Zion Church 18, 26
Allen, Frederick Lewis 2
Allen, Richard 18
Almstaedt, Isaac 63
American Baptist Home Mission Society 19
American Historical Association 1
American Revolution 38
American Social Science Association 74
Annals of Staten Island 23, 36
Arden Woods 72
Arthur Kill Road 48, 50
Askins, William 3, 23
Austen, Alice 69n
Azuka Street Movement 20

Beckmann, Frederick 13, 14
Baker, Tony 21
Barrett, Col. Nathan 12
Barrett, Nephews and Co.'s Fancy Dyeing Establishment 12
Bartlett, William Henry 52
Bayles, Richard M. 12
Bayne, Howard R. 114, 115
Bear, George 63

Bechtel, John 13
Bender, Thomas 78
Bennett, William James 52
Bethel African Methodist Episcopal Church 18, 21, 25
Billopp Conference House 41
Bischoff, Charles 14
Black Church 17, 18
Bongiorno, Joseph 3
Battle of the Boyne 98
Brace, Charles Loring 72, 100
Bradford, William 1
Brady, Mathew 59
Brennan, John 4
Brief History of the Settlement of Staten Island 1
Brighton Heights Reformed Church 126
Brooklyn 46, 63, 68, 83
Brooklyn Eagle 119
Brown, Chip 33, 34, 35, 43
Brown, Randall 3
Bryant, William Cullen 74
Bull's Head 9
Burbach, Jack
Burton, Katherine 98

Cartier-Bresson, Andre 44
Castle Garden 114
Castleton 12, 125, 126
Catholic Association 99

Catholic Emancipation Act 98, 99
Central Park 71, 74, 77
Chapman, John Gadsby 52
Charles II 9
Children's Aid Society 100
Chilton, Howard J. 58
Christ Church 126
Christian Methodist Episcopal Church 20
Church of God in Christ 20
Church of St. Andrew 63
Churches and Communities of Staten Island 27
Civil War 7, 10, 19, 53, 58, 74
Clifton 13, 52, 53, 59, 74
Clute, John J. 23, 36, 38
Colored Methodist Episcopal Church 19
Columbia College 1
Cone, James 20
Congregation of the Mission 99
Collins, Charles A. 119
The Conference House Revisited 37
Corrigan, Archbishop Frances 104
Cortelyou, Lawrence H. 50
Covell, Jane 2, 3
Crooke, John Jeremy 63
Cropsey, Jasper F. 48, 50
Cuestas, F. Vincent 21, 29
Cullen, Edgar M. 116, 119
Currier, Nathaniel 52
Curtis, George William 33, 35, 53, 74
Customs House 82

Dabrowski, Irene 2, 3
D'Arrigo, Charles J. 127
Davidge, Clara Potter 84
Davis, Mike 71, 78
Davis, William E. 125
Davis, William T. 37, 40, 41

Days Afield on Staten Island 40, 41
Dickenson, Richard 5, 20, 21, 23
Doherty, James 98, 100, 103, 105
Downing, Andrew Jackson 74, 78
Draper, John William 58
Drumgoole, Fr. John 4, 97, 99, 101, 102, 103, 105, 106
Dry Dock Savings Bank 9
Duke of York 9
Dutch Reformed Church 1

Eckstein, Monroe 1
Emerson, Hill 53, 87
Emerson, William 53, 74
Epps, William 28

Factoryville 57
Fein, Albert 77
First Church of God in Christ 25
Fisher, Irving 77
Flash, Edward 127
Fort Wadsworth 53, 57
Four Corners 14
Frank Leslie's Illustrated Weekly Newspaper 53
Free African Society 18
Fresh Kills 47, 48, 50

Garibaldi, Guiseppe 13
Gaynor, William J. 116, 119
Gleason's Pictorial 53
Gloster-Coates, Patricia 5
Great Kills 63
Greater New York 5, 27, 46, 117
Greenbelt 48, 76
Greene, Bradford M. 71, 75, 76
Grymes Hill 58

Haddad, Yvonne 29
Hamilton Park
Hammack, David 113, 118

Index

Hampton, Vernon 36, 39
Harper's Weekly 53
Harvard 81
Haynor, Anthony 3
Herring, Lucille 21
Hill, David 117
Hiss, Tony 71, 78
History of Plimooth Plantation 1
Horne, Field 37
Hoyer, H. 59
Huguenot 84, 85, 87, 94
Hunter, William 24

Irving, A.E. "Gugy" 127

Jackson, John 24
James II 98
Jarrett, Nathaniel, Jr. 29
Jersey Street 126
Jones, Absalom 18
Jonson, Ben 88

Keating, Edward 43, 48
King, Evelyn 21, 27
King, Martin Luther, Jr. 29
Klauber, Jacqueline 87
Kolff, Cornelius 35
Kreischer, Balthasar 7, 8, 9
Kreischerville 8

La Cerra, Charles 4
Lake, Bornt 36
Lake, John 63
Landfill
Landrum, Charles 21
Latourette 63, 84, 85, 87, 90
Leng, Charles T. 37, 40
Leo XIII 104
Loeffler, August 63
Loeffler, John 63

L'Ouverture, Toussaint 81, 90, 91, 92, 93
Lowell, Josephine 103

MacDowell Colony 83, 90
Manhattan 37, 44, 46, 50, 52, 57, 58, 68, 82, 97
Marchais, Jacques 87
Marchi, John 127
Mariners Family Home 52
Mariner's Harbor 9
McCloskey, John Cardinal 101, 104, 105
McMillan Harlow 38
Melyn, Cornelius 37
Melniker, Albert 3
Meucci, Antonio 13
Miller, W. R. 53
Mission of the Immaculate Virgin 97, 106
Molinari, Guy V. 33, 35
Morris, Ira 37
Morris' *Memorial History of Staten Island* 37, 112, 120
Metropolitan Compact 5, 33
Morton, Levi 117
Moses, Robert 3
Mount Loretto 97, 101, 104, 106
Mount Zion African Methodist Episcopal Zion Church 19, 24, 25
Muller Machine 113, 114, 115
Muller, Nicolas 114, 115
Mumpeton, Charles 8
Muralo Company 126
Murphy, John J. 127

Nakeeb, Diana 5
Napoleon 89, 90

National Association for the Advancement of Colored People 21, 28
National Baptist Convention of America 19
National Baptist Convention, U.S.A. 19
New Brighton 25, 35, 46, 52, 53, 57, 125
New Jersey 9, 11, 28, 57
New York Anderson Co. 9
New York City 34, 40, 111, 112, 117, 118
New York Dyeing and Printing Establishment 11, 12, 57
New Yorker 24
New York Times 34, 35, 43, 44, 46, 48, 65, 74, 82, 84, 88, 114, 115, 116
New York World 75
Nicholls, Richard 37
North Shore Colored Mission 25
North Shore Cycle and Benevolent Society 26
Novotny, Ann 69

O'Connell, Daniel 99, 105
Ogot, Bertham A. 20
Olmstead, Frederick Law 5, 52, 71, 72, 77, 78
Olmsted, John 73
Olmsted, Mary 73
Only Yesterday 2
Oyster Planters' Association of Richmond County 10
Ozanam, Frederick 100

Pavilion Hill 53
Pavillion Hotel 52, 126
Piels Brothers 14
Platt, Thomas 117

Pleasant Plains 97, 103
Plessy v. Ferguson 19
Perkins, Cyrus 73
Port Richmond 12, 26, 27
Potter, Frances 27, 28
Prince's Bay 9, 10
Proctor and Gamble
Progressive National Baptist Convention, Incorporated 19
Prospect Park 71, 74
Putnam's Magazine 74

Quarantine 39, 53, 59, 68, 69n

Randall, Robert Richard 111
Revolutionary War 13, 18
Richardson, H.H. 74, 75
Richmond County Democrat-Herald 33, 35
Richmond County Gazette 10, 11
Richmond County Mirror 52
Richmond County Sentinel 9, 14
Richmondtown 27, 37, 47, 50, 86
Richmond Terrace 46, 52, 63
Riley, Geraldine 4
Robertson, Archibald 50
Robinson, Edward Arlington 5, 81, 82, 84, 85, 86, 87, 88, 89, 90, 92, 93, 94
Rolph, John A. 52
Roosevelt, Kermit 82
Roosevelt, Theodore 82
Rosebank 4
Rosenfeld, Michael 4
Rossville 24, 52, 74
Rossville A.M.E. Zion Church 21, 24, 25, 28
Rubscam and Hormann 13, 14
Runkle, J.C. 127

Index

S.R. Smith Infirmary 14
Sachs, Charles 4, 35
Sailors Snug Harbor 2, 4, 52, 111, 112, 113, 115, 116, 119, 120
St. Andrew's Episcopal Church 86
St. George 27, 37, 47
St. John's University 2, 3, 4
St. Joseph's Union 97, 99, 103
St. Phillip's Episcopal Church 18, 25, 26, 27, 28
St. Vincent de Paul 99, 100, 101
Sandy Ground 3, 23, 24, 28
Sandy Ground Historical Society 20, 21, 23, 28
Sandy Hook 10
Seamen's Retreat 52, 53
Shaw, Albert 119
Sheperd, Barnett 3
Shiloah A.M.E. Zion Church 21, 24, 25, 27
Silver Lake 47
Smith, Christian
Smith, Dorothy Valentine 14, 37, 39
Society for Seamen's Children 52
Sorbonne 100
Stapleton 13, 25, 26, 52
Stapleton Union A.M.E. 19, 25
Starr, Roger 78
Staten Island Advance 20, 21, 26
Staten Island and its People 40
Staten Island During the American Revolution 38
Staten Island Historian 3, 24, 39
Staten Island Historical Society 41, 59, 65
Staten Island Improvement Commission 74, 77
Staten Island Institute of Arts & Sciences 4, 40, 59, 63, 71
Staten Island Lighthouse 85
Staten Island Patroons 37

Staten Island Railway 9
Staten Islander 58, 74
Steinmeyer, Henry 39
Sterne, Simon 112, 118, 119
Stuyvesant, Pieter 37

Tammany Hall 113, 114
Taylor, Henry 84, 88
Taylor, Yvonne 21, 28
Terrell, James 20
Thoreau, Henry David 53, 76, 87, 94
Tompkins, Daniel 3
Tompkinsville 25, 59, 63
Trask, Gustavus 112
Turner, Henry M. 19

Union Theological Seminary 19, 20

Vanderbilt, William 74
Van Pelt, Peter I. 1
Vaughn, John G. "Boss" 114
Vaux, Calvert 74
Verrazzano Narrows Bridge 4, 28, 38
Victory Boulevard 47
Virginia 10, 24
von Zimmerman, J.P. 76

Washington, James M. 19
Weber, Harvey 4
Weiner, Howard 4
West Brighton 12
White, William 18
Wilkins, Minna C. 24
Wooden, Lorentho 21

Yale University 72

www.ingramcontent.com/pod-product-compliance
Lightning Source LLC
Chambersburg PA
CBHW021845220426
43663CB00005B/412